W9-CZP-503

DAGGER

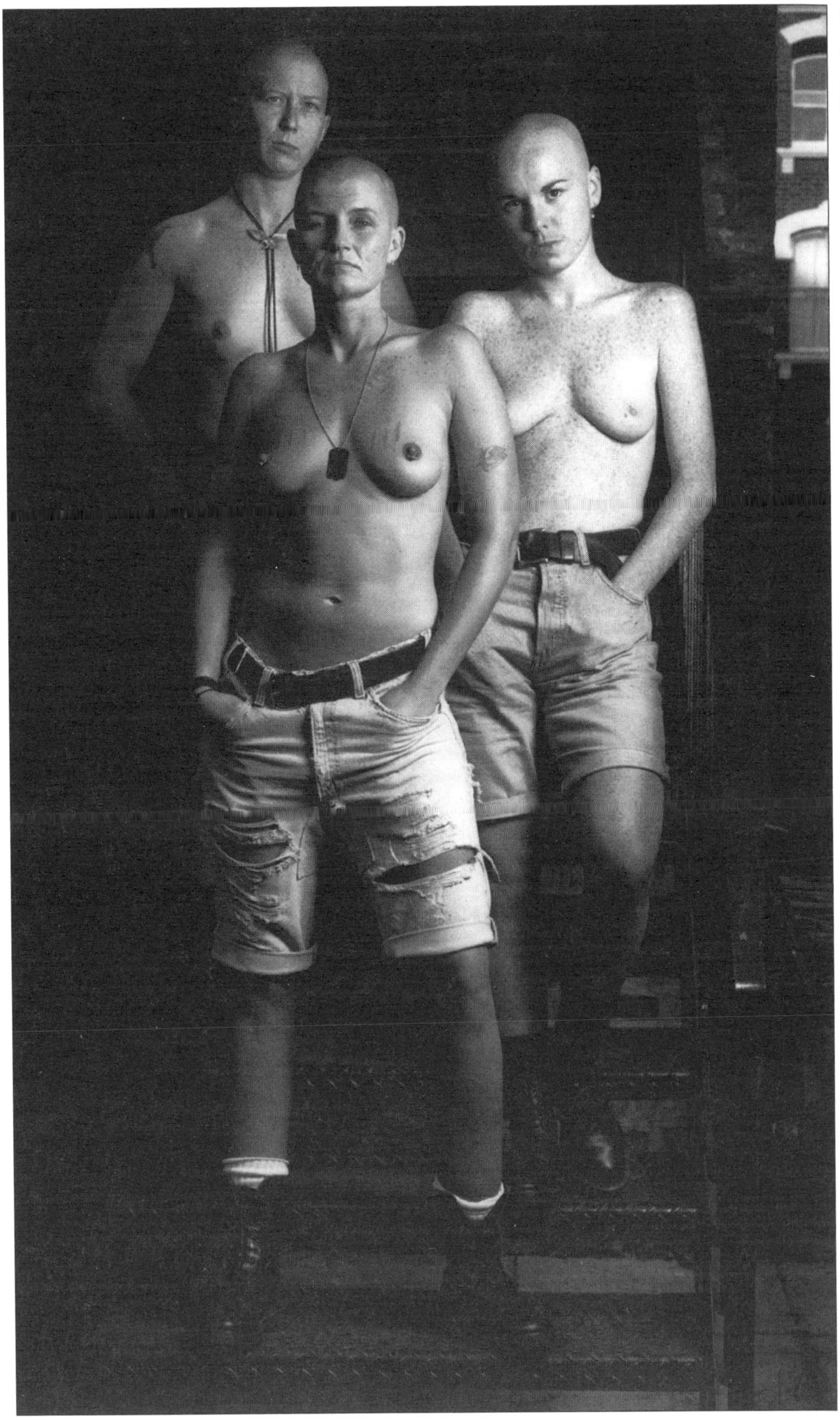

DELLA GRACE

DAGGER
On Butch Women

EDITED BY LILY BURANA ROXXIE LINNEA DUE

CLEIS PRESS

Published in the U.S.A. by Cleis Press, Inc.
P.O. Box 8933, Pittsburgh, PA 15221, and P.O. Box 14684, San Francisco, CA 94114

Book Design and Production: Peter Ivey
Cover Photograph: *Skeeter* © Della Grace

Printed in the United States of America
10 9 8 7 6 5 4 3 2 1
First Edition

Library of Congress Cataloging-in-Publication Data
Dagger : on butch women / edited by Lily Burana, Roxxie & Linnea Due.
— 1st ed.
p. cm.
ISBN 0-939416-81-6 (cloth) : $29.95. — ISBN 0-939416-82-4 (paper) : $14.95
1. Lesbians. 2. Sexual orientation. I. Burana, Lily. II. Roxxie. III. Due, Linnea A.
hq75.5.d34 1994
305.48'9664—dc20   94-2717
                                                                                CIP

GRATEFUL ACKNOWLEDGMENT is made for permission to reprint previously published material: An earlier version of "The Myth and Tradition of the Black Bulldagger" by SDiane A. Bogus originally appeared in *Black Lace*, Spring 1991; "Butch Desire" by Pat Califia originally appeared in *On Our Backs*, January/February 1992; "FTM: Female-to-Male" by Deva originally appeared in *Brat Attack* #3; "I Don't Think You Know What Butch Is..." ©1993 by Diane DiMassa; "Dyke Daddies" by Linnea Due originally appeared in *On Our Backs*, January/February 1992; "Daddy Boy Dykes" by Della Grace originally appeared in *Quim*, 1992; "Sex and the Single Gladiator" ©1991 by Donna Minkowitz; "The Wedding" by Genyphyr Novak originally appeared in *On Our Backs*, September/October 1993; "Sisters" by Caroline Ogg originally appeared in *Taste of Latex* #7, 1992; "Rosa Bonheur" ©1993 by Trina Robbins; "Crime and Punishment" by Cherry Smyth originally appeared in *The Advocate*, May 1992; "Confessions of a Dyke Daddy" by Jackie Weltman originally appeared in *Girljock*, 1992.

PHOTO AND ILLUSTRATION CREDITS: Lynn Breedlove–Tribe 8 © Anou; Kris Kovick and Her Dog, Two Femmes and a Butch Wearing Glasses, Elvis and Justin © Phyllis Christopher; Three Butches (standing), Three Butches (kissing), Queer Back, Lesbian cock, Daddy Boy Dykes ©1992 Della Grace; Two Butches Packing ©1986 Morgan Gwenwald; Greasing Up for the Dance ©1988 Morgan Gwenwald; J.C. ©1991 Morgan Gwenwald; Butched Up Barbie © Vicki Jedlicka; Butch Maxi-Pads ©1993 Andrea Natalie; two photographs accompanying the FTM discussion © Catherine Opie; Jill, eight years old (photograph by her mother, Charmian, 1961), The Balcony (San Francisco, 1988), Lisa and Lulu (San Francisco, 1989), Constance and Michele (San Francisco, 1993), Kitty (San Francisco, 1988), two photographs of Debra and Jane (London, 1988), Gina (San Francisco, 1993), April (San Francisco, 1993) © Jill Posener; Trash and Armand © Andrea Rodriguez; Butches Having a Smoke, Hulk, Winner ©1993 Yael Routtenberg; Basic Butch 101 from *Sharkmeat Comics* ©1992 Terry Sapp; for "Butch Icons of the Silver Screen" article: Shusuke Kaneko's *Summer Vacation: 1999* © New Yorker Films; Storme Delarverie © Sharon Farmer; *Flaming Ears* © Women Make Movies; *Adam Is Eve* ©1953 United Press Photo; *Times Square* © Associated Film Distribution; Sylvia Scarlett ©1935 RKO Radio Pictures, Inc.; for "Peppermint Patty and Her Sisters" article: *That Strange Girl*, D.C. Comics; *Hank*, Brenda Starr, The Chicago Tribune; *The Sensational She-Hulk*, The Sensational She-Hulk, Marvel Comics; *Rogue*, The Uncanny X-Men, Marvel Comics; *Big Barda*, Justice League International, D.C. Comics; *Maggie Sawyer*, Superman, D.C. Comics; *Amanda Waller*, Suicide Squad, D.C. Comics; *Rena Titañon*, Love and Rockets, Fantagraphics; *Doris*, Dynamite Damsels, Roberta Gregory; *Bitchy Butch*, Robera Gregory, Gay Comics; *Big Mean Sweaty Dykes Just Looking for Trouble*, Jen Camper, Gay Comics.

Contents

This book is dedicated to all the butches who paved the way
and to all the butches of tomorrow.

INTRODUCTION

WE BUTCHES could have had warning labels stamped on our foreheads as we emerged from the womb: *The identity that forms the core of your sexuality will be hazardous to your health.* Instead, we learned we were dangerous — and therefore in danger — in the old-fashioned way, from the backs of our mothers' hands, from taunts on the playground, from the way people looked at us with confusion and hostility. Half the time we didn't even know sex or gender roles existed; *we* were bad, not anything we were doing or would do.

Not much has changed since those days on the playground — not as we grow into adults or as we move forward in time. Consider these letters to *The Ladder*: "The kids in flyfront pants and mannish manner are the worst publicity that we can get," and "I think Lesbians themselves could lessen the public attitudes by confining their differences to their friends and not force themselves deliberately upon public notice by deliberate idiosyncrasies of dress and speech…. This is not fear or an imposed conformity, but a sensible courtesy." Frightened women in a frightening time: 1956 and 1957.

Update the phrasing, and those letters would fit in any gay paper today. Says Donna Redwing, an activist in the fight against antigay Measure 9 in Oregon: "When we started this campaign I thought we'd find a way to work together in a queer paradigm. But we got too scared. We excluded people out of fear — people wearing leather, transsexuals, people you see on the floats in San Francisco. We ended up marginalizing ourselves."

As two butches and one barracuda femme, we were adamant that our editorial policy exclude no one who had something to say about butch womanhood — but fear is still responsible for what's missing from these pages. Although we advertised everywhere for women to write us about being butch, looking butch, loving butch, we received few submissions we didn't dig for. We're so vulnerable in our lives that pinning ourselves to a page is terrifying — for those of us who have grown up dodging and ducking, standing still seems foolish. Guaranteeing pseudonyms wasn't enough. "Anyone can look at me and see what I am," one woman said as she refused an interview. "But if I say it, then it's on me." Even naming yourself to *yourself* can be scary — we duck and dodge inside, too.

So it's not surprising that those who are marginalized for other reasons were the ones who responded to our call. We heard from a butch sex worker in San Francisco, from a panel of female-to-male transsexuals, from dyke daddies. Humor lets us speak what we might otherwise not say, so we've collected cartoons, satiric pieces, and an examination of butch women in the comics. Our contributors write about growing up, about crossdressing, about our role models in popular culture. But we still haven't heard from the butch gardener in Houston, the dress-for-success CEO in Chicago, the crossdressing Filipina butch in Oakland. Despite these absences, we stress that butch is, more than anything else, about diversity, because we are *all* so very different.

Butch marries identity and sexuality. How could we not be idiosyncratic? Which is perhaps another reason we resist the label. A friend said she used to be butch. "I wouldn't let women touch me," she explains. "Now I do. So I don't qualify anymore." This woman was and is butch to her toenails, even when she's letting women make love to her — *especially* when she's letting women make love to her. She is being and caring for herself.

For butches, being butch is about being yourself; for society, being butch is about slapping convention in the face. When society is slapped, it strikes back — both at butches and at anyone else in the vicinity. A society which cannot tolerate genderbending or crossdressing ultimately will not tolerate homosexuality, bisexuality, or any other deviance from sexual or gender norms, no matter how closeted or assimilated. Butches are the cream that rises to the top of that pail of milk society would love to spill — or to gulp down in great draughts, the quicker to make us disappear. Butch women on the covers of popular magazines are thus absorbed into the general culture to be cast aside as yesterday's icon, or "mainstreamed" — stripped of sexuality and meaning, as if we were adherents to a quirky style, no more than a fashion statement.

Those who love us are equally beset by conflicts — the tie that was fun to tug on back at the apartment looks very different as you're approaching a crowded street corner — or even a lesbian bar.

What feels sexy when it's safe can so abruptly seem a lightning rod for outrage and affront. If we have to hide from ourselves and from our own community, who has the courage to confront the hostility on the street corner? Yet we do, every hour of every day, trying to explain who we really are. Each of us, those at the margins of gender and those who walk beside us, pick away at that sticky glue that keeps everyone mired in place.

Even as society would love to tame us, even as we ourselves are loath to name the invisible barrier that separates us from other people, we carry, merely by virtue of being ourselves, the seed of truth that gender is not an inflexible barrier, that, in fact, gender is much more permeable than we can imagine. Will we ever be ready to admit, as author Ellen Willis says, "that otherness is at bottom a defensive illusion"?

And here we must remark on a frequent complaint: "Can't we stop wasting our time dissecting butch/femme and get on with the important business of saving the world?" As much as we sympathize with the annoyance of those who believe we are mesmerized by our own navels, this particular criticism is nothing short of strange. Lesbians have been, are now, and will continue to be in the forefront of every progressive movement to grace this earth. We've tossed a number of causes into the public arena ourselves. But whether we're allowed to be visibly out while we're world-saving is another matter. We've been asked time and again to deny who we are — orientation, partner, dress and behavior — for the "good" of all these movements, our own unfortunately not excepted. We've been so adept at covering our identities that we've forgotten what freedom-fighters we have been.

Truly coming out — *Come as you are* — as part of a movement, as part of that queer paradigm Donna Redwing talks about, is as revolutionary as it gets. Nothing is more frightening than defining who we are in this time of siege because who I am can never be who you are, and who we are can never be who all of us are. No matter how hard we try to homogenize the lesbian nation, we are just as fractured — and just as full of vitality — as the rest of the world's peoples. What one of us calls co-option to a heterosexist mentality another sees as the act of a renegade. To defend our right to be visible, even when that very visibility puts us at risk, is courage born both of desperation and hope.

In a 1956 issue of *The Ladder*, the president of Daughters of Bilitis quotes a butch woman who is trying to assimilate: "I find that because now I am wearing women's slacks and letting my hair grow long I am getting a wider variety of friends and I have neighbors instead of people next door. I no longer have the feeling that everyone is watching me." *Dagger* is about women wanting others to see, about women claiming a name, about all of us carrying on in our diversity. It is about everyone watching us be ourselves.

LILY BURANA   ROXXIE   LINNEA DUE

San Francisco, December 1993

Why I Love Butch Women

CAROL A. QUEEN

I **DON'T** like smoking, but I'll put up with cigarette breath to watch a woman curl a lit butt into her palm like the Marlboro Man. I like femaleness — the curves, the wet spots — and I like femininity displayed, lace and lipstick and manicured nails, but it doesn't turn my head like worn Levi's and rolled tee-shirt sleeves, a stance like James Dean hustling on 42nd Street, the kind of womanness that isn't taught in school.

Simone de Beauvoir mused in *The Second Sex* that lesbian desire is related to desire for the mother, and that may be so, but honey, my mother was never like this:

Strong, I mean physically strong. Sexual, with a look in the eye that caresses and undresses. Attitude that comes from never fitting in, maybe from never even having tried.

Butch.

WHAT IS butch? Rebellion against women's lot, against gender-role imperatives that pit boyness against girlness and then assign you-know-who the short straw. Butch is a giant *fuck YOU!* to compulsory femininity, just as lesbianism says the same to compulsory heterosexuality. I do not associate respect for compulsory anything, in fact, with butchness, though perhaps some butch bottoms will disagree. I first gravitated toward butch women because they were the easiest female allies to recognize in my war against the compulsory world.

In the 1970s, when I came out into the dyke community, butch was dead and androgyny was practically an imperative. I didn't mind at first; girliness as a way of life hadn't worked out for me, and though I had always exhibited distinctly femme sexuality, I wasn't presenting myself to the world that way: I hadn't really grown into the image. I was young; the men I had fucked played "Me Tarzan, You Jane." I couldn't figure out how to get them to play the game by different rules. As soon as sex with them was over (or even while it was still going on), the whole thing felt stupid. Men who didn't play Tarzan were fine, but I couldn't figure out how to get them to fuck me. No doubt they were contending with their own straight (or not-so-straight) boy version of femme sexuality and were waiting for me to make the first move. Some men don't play Tarzan so as not to appear sexist; others just want you to do it — grab their neckties and put them where you want them — but I didn't know that at the time.

With some relief, then, I retired the Jane I never wanted to be, reconstructed myself as an androgyne, and forsook my vain attempt to present my femininity to the world. The Uniform, actually, was Butch Lite. Jeans or chinos, flannel shirts or tees, sensible shoes — either boots, athletic shoes, or Birkenstocks (it turns out the latter were incredibly subversive if you wore them with scarlet toenail polish, but that's another story). Almost the whole dyke community dressed this way: If a woman didn't, her politics and her sexual orientation were automatically open to debate.

The butches who were left over from the era before the purge also dressed this way. We had renamed the identity, it seemed, but kept the look. That way we could say we'd vanquished it, even as we kept it around to turn us on.

The unschooled eye couldn't tell the two sorts of women — butches and androgynes — apart. Butchness had been so thoroughly declared passé that an entire generation of dykes could dress in what was essentially butch-woman drag and evoke defensive responses only from conservative straight people (and very straight-identified "gay women").

At first I believed the mythos of the Vanished Butch (and her symbiotic sister-species, the Vanished Femme). But certain women wearing the Uniform made my nostrils flare, my tongue tie, my skin prickle like an electrical storm had passed. They filled the clothes differently. It took me some years to begin to understand why I wanted to chew on some women's thick brown leather belts and not on others.

Non-butch women wore the Uniform like librarians who had just come in from gardening. It was not clothes that made the woman. It was stance. It was attitude — it was impossible to picture one of the librarians wearing a tux, or myself dressing in silk or lace to present myself to her. It was impossible to think of presenting myself to her at all, to offer her that mixture of allure and willingness that I desired to give a butch woman.

The missing ingredient, I see in hindsight, was eroticism, worn on the sleeve and there in the step: Where political dykes would don a baggy flannel shirt and think, "No one will sexually objectify me if I wear this," the butches were tucking their shirts in, knowing that some little gal would love the softness of the flannel under her hands as she ran them up over the butch's pecs.

In that decade of butchness diluted and femme reviled, I had two lovers. Well, more than two, but only two who deserved *Lover* as a title, the way Radclyffe Hall called Una Troubridge *Wife* and Una called Radclyffe (whom she knew as "John") *Husband*. There were not then and are not now enough words to name what we wanted to do differently, or wanted to do the old-fashioned way, but queerly, with each other, like John and Una. We were lovers, not wives or husbands, living yet-unnamed relationships that had not fully evolved (though we tried so hard to speed the mired-down process of that evolution).

One lover was a butchette; how can I describe this? A femmey butch, I guess. Remember, we didn't talk this way then. Even reading Mary Daly together did not get in the way of our sex life. She was the most opinionated and assertive woman I've ever known, and though she did not fill out her clothes and went shopping the instant the Uniform lost its hegemony, she could lay me on my back more swiftly and skillfully than any woman has since. Though the seeds of my femme sexuality may have lain in abortive Tarzan and Jane scenes, it did not begin to blossom until our games of Sultana and captured princess. My lover oversaw that flowering: My own womanness had frightened me until the night we did Quaaludes, and I arched back off the bed, dizzy with the drug and a kind of power I had never relaxed into before, and purred: "I feel like Marilyn Monroe!"

To which she replied, hands full of me, "You *are* Marilyn Monroe."

A truly androgynous dyke could not have said such a thing.

She had committed quite a breach of lesbian-feminist etiquette (as, obviously, had I). Marilyn Monroe was a faggot's heroine, not a dyke's. We were not supposed to swoon over or identify with a woman whose femininity was her appeal and then her downfall, though Judy Grahn had already reappropriated Marilyn's thigh bone (by way of a poem) to bash in her enemies' heads: Hubba. Hubba. Hubba. (We didn't know that Grahn, as a butch, was thus privy to a more intimate vision of Marilyn than any self-respecting dyke was supposed to have, in those years before it came out that Marilyn had spent the early '50s getting her pussy licked by Lily St. Cyr.)

In celebrating my choice of Marilyn Monroe as spirit guide, my lover allowed my uncomfortable post-girly androgyny to cook away in the crucible of her arms, and to let me reconstitute as femme woman. It was a very butch thing to do. And it was very brave, because she was telling me I had her blessing in stepping off the path of political correctness; she was telling me that the wet truths of sex had our allegiance more fully, more instinctively, than the dry truths of lesbian feminism.

I love butch women because no one else would ever have reached into that flannel-clad bundle of inarticulate erotic yearning with a mirror that reflected a sex goddess. I love butch women because no one is quite so deeply affected by femme: I felt my sexual effect for the first time, and grew and grew like Alice in Wonderland drinking her magic potion. I love butch women because it was butch sexual response that gave me my body.

SHE CREATED a monster, of course. I could no longer be considered a right-thinking dyke. I was a lesbian crossed with a transvestite, sporting lingerie underneath my 501s. Oh, I know that's normal now, but then it was heresy. She bought me crotchless panties and untied the bows like I was a present that had been wrapped just for her, and before I melted into mindless throbbing waves of orgasm I had a political epiphany: Women who decried being objectified had

CAROL A. QUEEN

never had the opportunity to feel like this. They were an emblem of our sexual difference, those panties: We sinned, and shared our secret, together.

No one before her had paid such keen attention to my arousal, swooping down on my response like a claws-out hawk. In return I let her seize me, filled as full by her desire for me as by her cunt-slicked fingers.

What is butch? Sexual power of a kind that no woman is supposed to have, active power. Prowess. The calm eye of a whirlwind of pleasure, getting from giving. Learning the pure *skill* of giving a woman pleasure like no other soul can.

MY NEXT lover did "androgyny" so well that the night clerk at the first motel we checked into together winked at her and said, "Have a good time, Slim," never once thinking she might be a woman. Thinking about her reminds me of the injustice of the '70s claim that butch women were trying to ape male behavior to get "male privilege" (whatever the hell, in the hands of a woman, that is). This woman, like a lot of her sisters, couldn't have pretended to much of anything on the feminine side of the gender scale. Nineteenth-century German sex scientists named people like her *Sexuelle Zwischenstufen* ("sexually intermediate types"). And though there exists a photo of her at five with bows in her hair, by the time she was in her teens such affectations of girlishness were forever past: She had graduated to fast cars and drugs.

She had a low voice like honey mixed with whisky, not immediately recognizable as female, especially on the phone. She had muscles. She's the one who gave me my cigarette-curled-into-the-palm Marlboro Gal fetish. She was a loner who worked on cars. Getting her painfully-turned-inward attention seemed infinitely precious, for she was a woman who did drugs, took apart engines, and studied alchemy to forestall the need to dwell upon where she fit into the world.

Butch/femme, perhaps especially when unnamed, is a secret world. The basis of my powerful attraction to her was mysterious to me then, was chemical, and all the stronger for my inability to understand it. She was not the most devoted lover I ever had — far from it. There was too much sad-eyed stranger in her to ever get to know. She was barely domesticated, like the cat that spent its kittenhood wild; like simmering young Brando, ready to rebel against anything, even love.

My lover, so deeply Not-Feminine, came into her difference in a decade when what made her truly different from other dykes — real androgyny, perhaps born in the body, but certainly not politically chosen — was unnamed and less understood than it had been in any lesbian community in this century. To say her butchness was unsupported profoundly understates how alone she was in it; there was no discourse about it (except "It's dead"), and so the way she wore her lesbianism was denied, even — perhaps especially — by other lesbians. She had no mentors to teach her how to wear her difference — except men: But men could not teach her how a woman relates to another woman.

I knew I could never have the kinds of experiences she had had, never know what it would feel like to go through life in her body. I wanted to reach out to her difference and honor it, and I could do that by wanting her; I could do that by giving myself to her. No one in my world had fit in less and still survived, and I loved that in her.

CAROL A. QUEEN

I saw her as my shadow-sister, given an even more difficult path to walk than mine. But part of my difference lay in my willingness — no, my need — to love her.

Loving masculinity in a woman differs crucially in one way from loving it in a man: In her it is a badge of standing out, not of fitting in. It is grown into through pain, or at least a sense of separation from those less different.

What I love about butch women is their profound inability, or refusal, to be "normal." In the war between the sexes we can see them as warriors or resisters, but in any case, they stand as living proof that gender is more fluid, its imperatives more socially contrived and less innately rigid, than our conservative culture wants to allow. I love butch women for the same reasons the enigmatically gendered are revered in more enlightened societies than ours: Their very existence says that boundaries can be crossed. Like the spiritual and cultural respect some indigenous American peoples accorded the berdache, when I'm with a butch woman I feel awe at being allowed to see that the dualistic world is not as big as it gets. What I love about butch women is the way they stand as sentries, maybe even guides, to expanded possibility.

I'm aware I'm making this sound pretty existential, and for me it is, but I don't want to forget the sexual charge that surpasses respect and recognition, that moves my spiritual awe right to my cunt. When I'm sexing with a butch woman I'm consorting with a changeling, off mundane ground, like Wendy suddenly learning that all it took to fly was reaching for Peter Pan's outstretched hand. What makes me able to give myself like a precious gift to a butch woman, I think, is her understanding that I *am* a gift; what makes her know this, when other women miss it entirely, is part of the ineffable, the alchemical resonance between butch and femme that begins to heat the crucible. Standing far outside of traditional femininity, she finds in my femme-ness a representation of the un/familiar, which is just what she represents for me.

Yet if she were simply unfamiliar there would be less basis for the gift of self, less grounding for our passion; Tarzan and Jane don't recognize each other, and their desire emerges from their difference. Heterosexuals often face this obstacle: making cross-cultural attempts at intimacy without the knowledge of likeness-in-difference in which homosexual pairings, especially butch/femme ones, are grounded.

I believe we know too little about heterosexual love to know whether butch/femme relationships draw upon its premises or mirror it in any realistic way (I am not referring here to compulsory heterosexuality, which provides far too stifling an atmosphere for love and true fellow-feeling to flourish — real heterosexual love, a profound bond between socially constructed "opposites," is rare). Twin assumptions are that butch/femme mimics hetero bonding or, conversely, that it could have no relation to heterosexuality at all (since two women by definition are not heterosexual). I suspect that both butch/femme and hetero relationships share a sought-for balance between what is different and what is not, and difference is often eroticized. Butch and femme, though, experience their difference in like bodies; heterosexual difference is experienced in unlike bodies, embroidered to a greater or lesser degree by the cultural differences mandated by sex roles.

Most importantly, a butch/femme couple is queer. They do not meet social expectations even if they live exemplary role-differentiated lives — lesbians from "Leave It to Beaver." In fact, the more gender differentiation in their relationship, the queerer they are. In a heterosexual coupling, situated in this culture of hetero-hegemony, partners often live out their given roles unless mindful to do otherwise. In a butch/femme relationship the eroticized un/familiar exists not in the context of the normal, but of the forbidden.

What's considered normal is so fenced off from the multitudes of realities that confront and beckon us with their rich differences. The rigid boundaries that define "normality" have left it cut off and arid. The question "Am I normal?" has thwarted more orgasms, more wet cunts, more stiff dicks than any other single impediment to erotic bliss. Is it any wonder that I should embrace and adore those "not-normal" ones, the ones who wear on their sleeve their departure from the narrow, socially sanctioned path? I feel both inspired by their difference and safer in my own.

I love butch women because, in their big black boots, they step squarely across a line. I love butch women for the same reasons I love sissy men, the transgendered, the slutty, the outrageous queers of every stripe; the women and men who sell sex, and the ones who use sex to heal; the fetishists whose eroticism is more complicated than anyone ever let on to us eroticism could be. I love butch women because, in the face of ridiculously constricting gender

CAROL A. QUEEN

imperatives, they have the balls to say *Fuck it* — and to carve into our culturally empty space a different and powerfully confrontive way to live as a woman.

And that turns me on. Though I still can't altogether explain why my lover's "masculinity" was what aroused me, it's clear that I like masculinity better in women than in men! (Just as I love femininity better in men than in women.) My second lover's tales of teenaged fast-car adventure, the kinds of adventure I was never likely to have, got me incredibly hot. Hearing that she'd once driven a car through the wall of a house was not a stunt I wanted to repeat: It just made me want her to fuck me. The manifestations of our greatest difference, in fact, called up that response in me, as if fucking was the one way I could bridge our disparate experience. I think part of my sexual attraction to men stems from the same desire — to connect with that which I don't experience. But butchness is not the same as masculinity — it's a version of masculinity reflected in a wavy mirror, masculinity where our culture tells us not to look for it: in women, or in "macho" gay men, where a very male presentation throws a curve ball — a fey lilt to the voice or a hungry, up-raised butt. Loving butchness amounts to an attraction to what's not "supposed" to be there.

"Female maleness," "female masculinity": These simplistic ways of reading butch energy do not entirely miss the mark, but they do mislead. Maleness isn't male on a female, honey — it's something else again, a horse of another color, something our gender-impoverished language doesn't offer us words to describe.

I love butch women even if their butchness is nothing more than cussedness: "If there are only two ways to be in this world, I'll pick the other one." I love butch women because the alluring, unsettling power of their presence displays contempt for simplistic gender imperatives. I love butch women because they make straight people nervous. I love butch women because they resist. And even if I'm decked out in Frederick's of Hollywood fluff, if I'm on the arm of a butch woman, you can see that I'm a gender-resister, too.

A Random Sampling of Butches
Eight Questions Asked of Ten Butch Women

LILY BURANA

IF *I'd had an eternity to edit this book, I would have done full-length interviews with every butch woman I'd ever met, replete with personal histories, philosophies and juicy details. Daunted, but not deflated, by the reality of an eventual deadline, I abridged my full-length interview fantasy and called around to my butch friends — a wildly diverse lot, spanning the range of age, race, sexual preference and geographic regions — to do this anonymous, quickie, "just the facts" survey. Brief, but nonetheless informative. Think of it as an essentially topical look into some essential topics.*

MY BUTCH ROLE MODEL...

"James Dean."

"Jean-Claude Van Damme in *Hard Target*. OK, so he's a big, greasy macho guy, but with that haircut (spiked on the top, long in the back), he looks just like a dyke. Handles a weapon like one, too!"

"My Dad. He's the strong silent type, and so am I, for better or for worse."

"My Dad. He's a fag, and by being out, he has taught me to be honest about who I am."

"Faggots."

"Grace Jones. She's the butch version of Arsenio Hall."

"My aunt Pat. She was the first dagger I ever knew. Too bad she
    died before I came out as butch."
"Marlon Brando in *The Wild Ones*."
"The Fonz from 'Happy Days.' He inspired my Neanderthal side."
"The butches from the earlier part of this century. Their courage and
    style are impressive."

BUTCH FASHION MUSTS...

"Levi's 501 jeans."
"White tee-shirt."
"Tuxedo, if you're a glamour butch."
"Black leather boots."
"A little red dress, just to keep people on their toes."
"Black leather jacket."
"A well-pressed dress shirt."
"A dark suit."
"Boxer shorts. Plaid cotton for casual, silk for makin' whoopie."
"Chaps."

BUTCH FASHION CRIMES...

"Leisure suits."
"Anything pink."
"Ruffled dress shirts."
"Plaid golf shorts."
"Bell-bottoms."
"Girls' clothes."
"Polyester."
"Men's — or women's — thong bikini underwear."
"Birkenstocks."
"Spandex tights, except for sports."

COOL BUTCH NAMES...

"Terry, Randy, Sid, Lou, Mel. Anything that could be for a man or
    woman or can be shortened to a man's name."
"Rex."
"Javier."

"Just using initials is nice… J.B., R.J., etc."
"Jake."
"Mike."
"Spike."
"Butch."
"Ace."
"Charlie."

BAD BUTCH NAMES...

"Egbert. No explanation needed."
"Roger."
"Francis. Too soft."
"Dick."
"Butch. Too obvious."
"Sir Clitoressa."
"Sue."
"Orville."
"Dude."
"Barney."

My Early Life as a Butch Was...

"Confusing. My mother wanted a daughter, and my father wanted a son, so I went from dresses to pants all the time. My father ended up happier with my outcome, that's for sure."

"Uneventful, until my first love dumped me for the captain of our high school football team and told everyone I was gay."

"Cool. I had three brothers and was a total tomboy and then a jock. My family was even OK when I came out at the age of sixteen."

"I hated being a kid. I felt like a boy, but was forced to wear dresses until I was ten and had the misfortune of being named Jennifer. I made people call me Jay and still do."

"Hard. My dad kicked me out of the house when I refused to 'quit being a tomboy and look like a real woman.' Luckily, I came to the city and made friends with a bunch of queers who took me in and introduced me to the queer way of life."

"Strange. I was popular, but considered weird. People nicknamed me 'butch,' but I didn't like it."

"I got harassed a lot when I was younger, especially by white, presumably straight men who were threatened by a young, masculine-looking woman of color."

"As a really young child, I had crushes on girls in my school and my female teachers. As a teenager, I wanted to go to the prom in a tux with a girl on my arm, but I felt that would be unwise for either myself or my girlfriend."

"I felt really alienated most of the time, except when I was involved in athletic things. I got a lot of respect for being a good athlete in school, until I dropped out."

"I can't remember much of my early childhood, but I can't say my teen years were so great. Beer and pot were staples of my diet, because I didn't have any other way to cope with who I was — I later learned it was called being butch — in a small midwestern town."

A Low Point of Being Butch...

"Being out with my femme girlfriend and watching straight men hit on her, even though it's clear she's with me."

"Having someone look at me and say, 'What the hell is THAT?!'"

"Figuring out which public restroom is safer for me to use — the men's or the women's."

"Trying to make use of a cheap, floppy dildo."

"Feeling like a freak in the feminine hygiene aisle. All those pastels piss me off. When will they invent a butch maxi pad?"

"Trying to find a bra. My tits are too big to go without one, and I look like an absolute idiot in those frilly, lacy numbers."

"Not knowing whether or not I should be flattered when a stranger says, 'Excuse me, Sir.'"

"Telling a woman I'm not interested in being penetrated sexually. Most women look at me like I'm helplessly old-fashioned. I'm not, I'm just not into it."

"Wearing pantyhose and a women's suit to work. I feel like I'm in bad drag."

"Encountering people who equate being butch with being a pig."

A HIGH POINT OF MY BUTCH LIFE...

"Marrying my lover at the March on Washington. It made it all real!"

"Winning my first marathon in middle school. It was the first time I was validated for being strong."

"When I found another butch who was into butches. I thought I was the only one."

"Riding down the street on my bike one day. It wasn't any special occasion, I just suddenly realized how right and powerful I felt!"

"Walking down the street with a pretty girl on my arm and watching everyone turn around to look at her and seeing she's with me."

"Finally realizing that there were women who were attracted to me because of, not despite, my being butch."

"My first love. I was thirteen, she was eleven. She lived in the next building, and one night I convinced Mama to let her sleep over and I seduced her right on my bedroom floor!"

"Having a gay man hit on me, not realizing that I was a woman! You know you can pass when...!"

"Seeing butch and femme once again celebrated as a valid, vital choices for dykes. There were so many years when we were considered unconscious dinosaurs."

"When I figured out how to pee standing up."

The Myth and Tradition of the Black Bulldagger

SDiane A. Bogus

THERE is really no such thing as a Black lesbian; well, not in the African-American past anyway. The word lesbian is a derivation of the Greek word *Lesbos*. Lesbos was an isle of Mitylene, Greece, where sixth-century songstress and poet Sappho was supposed to have trained, loved, and instructed young ladies in the arts of music, composition of verse, dancing, and love.

Like the ideal of the Black woman as immemorial African queen in the high literature of Black poets and writers, Sappho has arrived in the twentieth century royally imagined and adored as an ideal lesbian by contemporary women-loving women of all colors. The fact is, if one calls herself a lesbian at all it is because Sappho was from Lesbos, and hence the circumlocutions of etymology.

Although she is heralded in countless lesbian poems, essays, books, artistic representations, rituals, and conversations — in which she is portrayed as a fair-skinned nymph whose genteel and aesthetic woman-loving woos women to visions of lyre music and nimble-footed dancing under nature's fullest moons — Sappho is not our highest, truest or best representation.

Sappho doesn't have enough historical, romantic, or physical substance to make her as rich as our own culture makes the Black Bulldagger (whom I distinguish from the Black lesbian). Sappho isn't American or African-American. This is a distinction of nationality and culture, not of race, for Sappho, as a Greek, was probably a woman of color. Judy Grahn, in *Another Mother Tongue,* has described her as "small and dark." Obviously this is not well-disseminated information; in fact, it is ignored, as is the obvious dark skin of the historical Jesus, who nonetheless hangs on the cross lily white, stained with red, red blood. As in Jesus's case, Anglo-heterosexual and homosexual culture has created Sappho in the image of a white deity much like Venus or Artemis (Diana) whom Sappho and the girls of Mitylene worshipped. I can respect this lesbian past and understand the necessity of bringing it forward to these times, times in which any historical evidence of homosexual lives is (for all of the visibility of gays and lesbians) still rejected or denied. We must be fastidious about preserving lesbian and gay history, but as a Black lesbian feminist, I am annoyed by the ethnocentric racism inherent in advocating for the symbol of One Lesbian. In this the herstory of Black lesbians is made invisible by omission.

The images that are put forth of women-loving women, Amazon women, are rarely women of color. Yet we accept these images as symbolic of our loving; we often subscribe, whether consciously, resignedly, or willingly, to the idealism of these images, all the while being defined by them. This essay is an attempt to revitalize the sense of self and history that the Black lesbian must maintain, develop and nurture if she is to survive as a reality and as a teacher for the next generation of women-loving Black women.

AFRICAN-AMERICAN lesbians have, in our ancient lesbian past, the fierce Dahomean Amazons of West Africa who were, during the Songhai influence over that region (1464–1591), the most learned, the richest, and the most sought-after people on the planet, if not for their knowledge and riches, then for their slaves. These were Amazons, as Audre Lorde wrote in *The Cancer Journal,* who severed their right breasts in order to free their bow arms for the fight against enslavement. We also have Queen Califia, namesake of California who, according to legend, was a thirteenth-century leader of a tribe of Black Amazons who ruled the land without the presence of a single man.

The Black Bulldagger is a link to our ancient and recent Black woman-loving past, and the predecessor of today's Black lesbian. She is a character, an idea, a woman who loved women but was

SDIANE A. BOGUS

heavily male-identified more often than not. She was the unattractive girl, the tomboyish teen, the independent woman, or any Black sister who repulsed the advances of men.

Moreover, the Black Bulldagger, unlike the Black lesbian, was a loner in both myth and reality. She had no politic other than her daily life. She had no community other than that which she discovered. She had no women-loving role models other than men. She had no books, no records — save those that she hid — no café (unless you include the out-of-the way bar or the house party), and she had no festivals. But the Black Bulldagger survived in our language, in our imaginations, and in our lives. If we were to assign her an era, that era would begin in the 1880s and extend through the 1950s. The 1920s were her best years.

The Black Bulldagger's American antecedents were women such as gun-toting Mary Fields (1832) or Cora Anderson (1840) who passed as male and married a woman. She even had intellectual counterparts who were less assertive Black women-loving women than she. They include Alice Dunbar Nelson and Angelina Weld Grimké, the artistic branch of the women-loving line. But the Black Bulldagger is not an artist in our imaginations. She is a creature made in the image of man. She is the doorway through which many of today's conveniently labeled Black lesbians have passed as studs, as "sweet-men."

The Black Bulldagger has also been women like Ma Rainey and Bessie Smith, Mabel Hampton, and Annie Lee Grant, a Mississippi bulldagger who lived as a man for fifteen years. Through eight decades, the presence of the Black Bulldagger has waned but has never disappeared.

Know that we come to the Black Bulldagger with some confusion. She has existed and does exist; she is both a folk myth and a genuine article. She has been a transvestite, a bisexual, and always an identifiable lover of women. We've seen her and have not seen her; we've heard about her or whispered about her. The Black Bulldagger has been what our girlhoods abhorred: we the ribbons; she the hat. We the dolls; she the jack. We the prom; she the bar. We the wife — the protectorate of man, his mistress, girlfriend, or date; she the woman-made-woman, her self's own escort, her own self's counsel and chief, the equal of men.

In this she is very unlike Sappho, for Sappho, in the end, is an ambiguous figure, very distant in time and very much the image men most prefer in Woman: the delicate beauty in silks, harmless, hardly man's equal even if she knows a million thrusts of the *olispo* (dildo). Sappho is the lesbian men want to watch in movies. They want to see airy-fairy, wispy strokes and caresses between women, the imagined frustration of penis-less tribadism. They want to see breast sucking and cunt tickling because, to them, therein lies no consummation. The Black Bulldagger would never give them a show, and no one would ever know the ways of her loving. What skills she had with women, what art, what pleasures in her hands, what practice in her tongue, whatever augmentations to her desire, she never told. She kept her own council. She went for bad.

THE STRENGTH of the Black Bulldagger lies in the self-asserting herstory of our pasts. Any Black woman with character enough to cry, "Look at my arm! I have ploughed, and planted, and gathered into barns, and no man could head me! And ain't I a woman?" has the same power or potential for power as the Black Bulldagger. She, like Sojourner Truth, has had to struggle for her place in our minds, against our weakness and fear, our fuzzy sense of our lesbian past, our Black history, and against internalized homophobia. But because we have not seen her humanity, nor her loving, and have only begrudged her strength, power, and woman-loving nerve — we cried out "Bulldagger! Bulldagger!" hardly knowing the words were an incantation to our own hidden Black histories.

BULLDAGGER. JUST what does this word mean? Where does it come from? It is related, as Judy Grahn speculates in *Another Mother Tongue*, to Boudica (*Boo-dike-a*), the Iceni Queen of Celtic history who rode on Rome against the colonization. In AD 61 she reigned as priest-goddess and queen, performing ceremonial rites wherein bulls were regularly killed on the altar of sacrifice. The blood ran down into a embankment or "dike" that drew it away. In any case, her descendants and others like them gave to lesbians a character rebellious, armed, masculine, warrior-like, and dangerous. Boudica's name, like her wondrous but infamous defiance of Rome, was driven underground, not to be spoken, not to be remembered except with derision: "bulldiker, bulldagger, Boudica."

The name Boudica and the business with bulls and dikes accounts nicely for the associative transposition to bulldiker, but Boudica's name doesn't quite account for the use of it in Black culture. Our Bulldagger is said to have sexual prowess beyond the wildest dreams of a man, and certainly beyond his damnedest capabilities. How did this Iceni legend arrive in Black culture? Or is bulldagger some wild concoction of the Black imagination?

Before the Roman Empire, was that of ancient Egypt. Subduing bulls or sacrificing them is as old as Horus, the bull, Egyptian ruler, consort to (Black) queen Tyre. It is in our blood. Come from northern Africa as certainly as the Black and female sovereignty of Neferititi, Hatshepsut or Cleopatra.

Ancient Egypt, the land of the Great Sphinx, of hieroglyphics, mummification, treasures, and unknowable mysteries. All that is in our blood if not in our accessible memories. Our reverence for, fascination with, interest in the bull is as honest as the day we were born; it is as old as the word "God" or "El," which, according to *The Woman's Encyclopedia of Myths and Secrets*, means "bull god or Father of Men." And it was Bill Pickett, Black cowboy extraordinaire, whose magnificent and creative rodeo feats with bulls reminded us of our connection to the ancient relations of Blacks and bulls.

In the 1920s, Black people who had migrated from the Midwest farms and southern parts of the United States to the North had the rare and uplifting treat of seeing Bill Pickett in the one and only movie of its Black kind, *The Bulldogger*. There he was on the great silver screen, larger than life, leaping from horses with the greatest of ease, wrestling bulls and calves to the ground in record time, manhandling them in the most rope-fangled fashion, and creating for the new American West a rodeo event that lives on today. His feats credited him with the origin of the word "bulldogger." The word was then appropriated by other cowboys who had observed the behavior of bulldogs who'd get a hold of something and refuse to let it go.

Once we had seen that movie, we talked about Bill Pickett, and we talked about his exotic life, and we said "bulldogger" whenever we could. We used it as a term of reference for any man's prowess, especially if he was bullish about women; we created similes using "like a bulldogger" to describe how fiercely, adroitly, or strongly a task was performed. The word "bulldogger" had its way with our imaginations. Then somewhere, at some time, somebody crossbred that admiration with hate, or with comedy, when he saw one bull mount another and go heigh-ho in forceful stabling motions, or when some woman did a thing with the unabashed aptitude of a bulldogger. In the twinkling of an eye, or perhaps, in the time it takes to spread gossip, the word "bulldogger" became "bulldagger."

Bulldagger. Just what has it come to mean? Ask any contemporary Black lesbian, and she'll tell you. It means ridicule; it means you act like a man, that you go for bad, that you're some kind of freak, and that you hate men. She is a hellish "It," a supernatural "he," or at the very least, an "unnachel" woman. And she was, even to herself, the most despicable beast in the hell of a man's world. In Black oral tradition, especially in old wives' tales, the Black Bulldagger is and has always been a creature of enormous power to those who were terrorized by the tales of her knife-toting ways, her smooth charm, her exceptional and extraordinary sexual parts. Her clitoris was called "a hammer" or "a pertongue" (or pearl tongue). It was thought to be elongated, a very different organ between her legs which could hook onto a woman's libido and enslave her heart or ruin her health. Once taken from a man, a Bulldagger's woman would never go back again. These are the myths, but the reality was that the Black Bulldagger believed she had a right to love women, and she lived that right fearlessly. She believed she had the right to walk the streets day or night unmolested, and she did — conquering the fear in her heart. She believed she had the right to defend herself and her chosen, to assert herself, to govern herself.

The Black Bulldagger did not lack the courage of her convictions. She was self-defining, self-escorting, self-reliant; she was proud, manly, possessive, and strong; she was streetwise and recognized for herself when she wanted to be. The attributes of the Black Bulldagger are not all complimentary or worthy of emulation; not all are applicable to the evolved Black lesbian. To distinguish ourselves, to distinguish our way of woman-loving, we must begin to ask ourselves what there is to be saved in the model of the Black Bulldagger. At present we lose much by our estrangement from her. It is true that our woman-loving style may be less possessive, less male-identified, more equal in sexual exchange and in the power dynamic, but are we as well-defined, as relentlessly public (i.e. free), or are we still constrained by the horrors of being called "bulldagger!" Is it easier to be called a dyke or to be enveloped in someone else's image of ourselves?

As Black lesbians who are on the threshold of the twenty-first century, we must repossess as much as we can of our woman-loving past to shore us up for the future. We can no longer allow our lesbianism to be defined for us by popular ideology, by the non-Black lesbian ideal — though some non-Black heroines may embody our values. As Black lesbians we are certainly less threatening and threatened than ever a Bulldagger was. We have a freedom of being that she never had. I propose we find ways to repossess the model, the lessons, and the power of this unlikely matriarch.

Sex and the Single Gladiator

Is a Ridiculous TV Show Sparking a Revolution in Sexuality?

DONNA MINKOWITZ

These people are one notch above humankind, and we want to show off what unbelievable bodies they have.
— "American Gladiators" producer Brian Gadinsky

IT'S the start of the Tarzan competition. The iron-thighed female gladiators anchor themselves atop fifteen-foot plastic pillars. Athletic but less brawny female amateurs swing in on ropes in the wild hope of toppling them with their bodies. The moment of impact is the only woman-to-woman moment on TV that makes me hold my breath; it's not every day that straight tube lets you watch a thin tomboy from Dubuque trying to knock a stronger woman to the ground.

The contest looks nothing like those "Hot Fighting Broads" entertainments intended solely for men. A woman with biceps as big as Ice the Gladiator's and a steely expression to match can't be turned into your average giggling mud wrestler babe too easily. Those shots of hard female bodies colliding are a thousand times more Joan Nestle than Howard Stern. Forget "LA Law"; if ever there was a TV show for lesbians, it's "American Gladiators."

The male athletes on "American Gladiators" give good spectacle, too, but that wasn't the reason I hightailed it to the show's New York tryouts at the Coliseum — the idea of two thousand women jocks in shiny athletic togs burning to cream some faux-Roman musclewoman was. Like so many others, I'm drawn to "AmGlad" because it's the only TV show where women with big muscles are celebrated as the living gods they are — as opposed to, say, "In Living Color," where a male actor plays a hideously ugly female bodybuilder who applies force to her breasts to make them shrink. "We're proud of women's body building and of their physiques," says "AmGlad" producer Brian Gadinsky. "One of the things that attracted me to the show in the first place is that there *is* equality, with the same number of men and women competing."

But first, you have to teach enough young girls that it's OK to have a forearm that could choke a horse. Sadly, the lineup of contender wannabes outside the Coliseum boasts few women of that description. Instead, male applicants outnumber females by about four to one, and most of the women are lightweight runner types in spandex, not tricep queens or even beefy girls in Army tees. Many of them do have tattoos, though. The boys on line are an infinitely more swaggery sort, showing off their tiger pants and doing unnecessary stretches so the rest of the crowd can see their lissome quads. I get all choked up seeing women on line with their infants and young children — I envision impassioned demos about childcare for musclegirls — but they all turn out to be noncontenders waiting for their men. The favorite female hairstyle on line is long, blond, and puffy, like a heavy-metal rocker's date.

But some butch items *do* make it to Columbus Circle in time to save me from utter disappointment. Melinda, a white woman with biceps from angels and merry orange sweatpants, looks like every hot dyke on the Yale women's rugby team, iron-torsoed and friendly with the knowledge of how sexy that iron is. "I like the challenge," she says with wonderful jock triteness. "I want to show the gladiators we can be tough, too." She exults just as cheesily as the men when she passes the chin-up test, slapping her friends' hands and grinning the easy grin of a woman with upper body strength.

A black woman with massive forearms and the dignified air of a Marine strides to the chinning bar, making me wonder why I passed up the GI Outreach Committee at the last antiwar confab. At the forty-yard dash, a beautiful, six-foot-tall, apparently transsexual bodybuilder in purple leggings and a gigantic floral bra is having the time of her life out-racing all other contenders. "I think this is good publicity for women and what they can do," she tells me. "Women can do anything!"

For the women who successfully get through the chin-ups, forty-yard dash, and rope climb, the last and most difficult test of powerball at the Coliseum tryouts is a one-on-one *mano-a-mano* with only one basket. Rosann Torres, a twenty-three-year-old dark-haired number whose arms are packed with muscle, says she's trying out because on "American Gladiators," "you get to show how athletic you are, and you get to go to California and get a tan." Here, Torres gets to tackle and keep tackling a wispy blonde with a tattoo. The blonde seems completely mismatched — but maybe the organizers planned it that way. The blonde keeps on losing, Torres keeps tackling her, and I don't know if I'm watching a sport or reading Pat Califia.

She has her legs clamped tightly around the legs and lower torso of the flailing contender. Both are dangling in mid-air above the heads of hundreds of gaping watchers, suspended only by hand-grips. The thin girl struggling on the rings is being loudly and patronizingly coached by her contender-husband from below, but now the results of his coaching are becoming clear: No way can she escape the hard-bodied Ice. As the girl writhes and tries to hold on, Ice's legs scissor her down to the ground. "I had one hundred and fifty-seven pounds on her!" laughs the blond gladiator.

THIS LITTLE vignette really happened during a recent installment of "AmGlad," but only the VCR replay button made me confident I had actually watched it and not just fantasized it. Are the gladiators aware they stimulate the gonads quite so much?

That's what I asked when I had breakfast with the meanest gladiator herself the morning before the tryouts. "The show is totally sexual," confirmed Ice, aka Lori Fetrick, a twenty-eight-year-old Pasadena native who's been a bodybuilder for six years. "That's part of the entertainment value. When you have these health-conscious people in skimpy outfits, sure people are going to get turned on."

Fetrick also seems to enjoy her threatening image. She says she chose the name Ice because "I love the name 'Iceman' from *Top Gun*. It sounds very cool, and very *intimidating*." She uses the I-word so much she could be Jean Genet kvelling about rough men. "These girls come on the show and take one look at me, and my appearance is very intimidating. I am the biggest woman on the show, and they say, 'Oh my god, she's terrifying!'" The other gladiators joke that she is "cold as ice," Fetrick, exuding warmth, adds happily.

The woman who regularly pulls strong girls off an artificial wall against their will formerly worked as a personal trainer and corporate sales rep ("can you imagine me behind a desk, nine to five?"), and becoming a gladiator fulfilled a few important fantasies of her own. "It's been my lifelong dream ever since I was a child to be a professional athlete. For women, there's not a whole lot we can do as a way to break in and make a living as physique stars." Soon Fetrick hopes to go pro as a bodybuilder in the National Physique Committee, a part time gig that would still leave time for intimidating contenders before national TV audiences.

Meanwhile, Fetrick notes that being on "AmGlad" takes the bite out of society's general dissing of pumped-up women. "The general public feels funny when they see how I look," she observes. "But once they find out I'm on 'American Gladiators,' they don't care. If there were any negatives, it's gone."

Her message to the audience at home? "There must be some rough, tough girls out there who think 'Ice is no problem,'" the blue-eyed, iron-thighed one singsongs. "So I say, 'Come on, babe, let's go.'"

Can a ridiculous TV show spark a revolution in the way people perceive girls with pecs? They say all social change begins with fantasy, and already for women athletes, butch is suddenly in and Wonder Woman is out. Maybe "American Gladiators" could inaugurate an era of whole-hog toleration for both sensuality and silliness. Like dig this explanation of the gladiators' skimpy costumes, from no less an authority than gladiator Gemini, aka former Patriot and Eagle player Michael M. Horton: "There's no sense in dressing people with great bodies in full body sweats." (Now imagine if he'd said that while still playing pro football.) On the show a couple of weeks ago another hunk gladiator, Nitro, boasted he was about to give the male contenders "the big gladiator spanking." Didn't they wish.

Ice, Gemini, and I sit in a lounge overlooking the tryouts,

discussing the show's sexual impact. "I don't think we do anything intentional to make the show sexy," says Gemini.

"*I* do!" Ice interrupts. "Just kidding," she teases, but I doubt it.

I have to choose one of three doors to run through at top speed in hopes that a gladiator isn't behind it. I choose one and run, but lean, dynamic, African American Blaze is behind the door, and she tackles me to the ground…. I'm pummeling brawny but busty Lace with a twenty-five-pound padded pugil stick, and she's pummeling me back…. Then I grab a lanky athlete off a fake mountain as my helmet cam records her valiant but ultimately futile effort to hang on….

Could this be the sport that makes lesbian imagery cool, once and for all?

JILL AGE 8, PHOTOGRAPHED BY HER MOTHER

Photographing Butch

JILL POSENER

Jill Posener is a British photojournalist whose work has been published internationally in publications ranging from On Our Backs *to* The New York Times *and* The Village Voice, *and in anthologies like* Stolen Glances, *a lesbian photo collection. She has published two collections of photographs of political graffiti,* Spray It Loud *and* Louder Than Words (*Pandora Press*).

THE photographic process for me is a type of seduction. Not a sexual seduction, but a process of asking and coaxing someone to reveal herself, reel by reel. I find it hard to ask a butch to reveal herself because it makes me feel vulnerable. Perhaps I'm uncomfortable with even the hint of a sexual dynamic being present with another butch – and there can be a sexual aura during a photo shoot. It's less threatening for me to ask a femme to be more daring, more explicit, and though I am attracted to femme women, there is less of a sexual charge during a photo shoot. I wish I had more rapport with butches because I love to photograph them and I'm always excited by the results.

People have said that I've been experimenting with genderfuck for years in my work. I've always resisted that. I am ambivalent about the issue of gender dysphoria, the idea of gender fluidity. I'd like to photograph the process of someone's transition from female to male, but I admit I would feel like a voyeur. My fascination with something I don't fully understand or empathize with might be a barrier. Or it might not; it might allow for a cooler, more practical approach.

Photographers are always playing out in their minds how something will translate into a solid image. We are observers and voyeurs. There was a film from Finland in the San Francisco International Lesbian and Gay Film Festival about a female-to-male transsexual. It was beautiful and riveting. But what it said to me was that to make the transition to becoming a man you had to want one thing: to be among men as a man. You had to love maleness. I realized that was the antithesis of what I had always wanted as a butch. That being butch for me was essentially about loving to be with women — despite my discomfort about some aspects of being a girl when I was growing up: the clothing, the menstruation, the breasts.... Butch has been the identifying feature in my life since I was about eight years old when my Mum bought me my cowboy outfit and photographed me in it, surrounded as I was by rather pretty girls.

Photographing butch is hard. I certainly would resist any photographer who wanted to photograph me for a book on butches. Butches are isolated and vulnerable. This isn't a period of celebrating butch/femme identity.

I know in my own work the process of asking a butch to reveal herself in front of the camera brings up the sense of being even more exposed in a world which has held our image up to ridicule. I am scared of continuing that. So I love it when butches emerge from the photos as completely at ease with their identities.

Sometimes I apply my own skewed sense of modesty, my own discomfort. If someone unzips her jacket a little too far and her breasts are revealed, I have a hard time resisting the temptation to cover them up.

JANE AND DEBRA

JANE AND DEBRA

KIM AND MICHELE

APRIL

LISA AND LULU

THE BALCONY

KITTY

JILL POSENER

GINA

Crime and Punishment

Alleged Male Impersonator Says Prison Is a Dyke Paradise

CHERRY SMYTH

JENNIFER Saunders, the seventeen-year-old who became an international lesbian celebrity after a British judge sentenced her to six years imprisonment for allegedly impersonating a man to have sex with women, has been released after serving nine months of her sentence. After her punishment was reduced to a two-year suspended sentence by an appeals court on June 12, Saunders, finally able to speak with her supporters, described prison as a dyke paradise and explained that she had concocted the bizarre story that landed her in jail to protect her lovers.

Saunders's case reads like a surrealist movie script. The suit against her was brought by the parents of two women who had been Saunders's lovers, Rebecca Andrews, then fifteen, and Helen Edwards, then sixteen. The women told the court in Yorkshire, a working-class region in northern England, that Saunders had passed herself off as a young man named Jimmy who had a cancer on one side of his chest and a boil on the other and could not allow his penis to be touched because of an operation he'd had. The relationship with Andrews, according to the trial transcript, lasted five months, during which Saunders "penetrated R. with an object on over twenty occasions." Edwards was said to have been penetrated once with "a sharp, rough, and thick object."

Though Saunders did not deny the allegations during her original trial, she and Adrian Fulford, a gay lawyer who handled her appeal, now maintain that both women were aware that Saunders was a lesbian.

"Both women had consented and were willing participants," says Fulford.

"She knew I was a bird [British slang for woman] and that she was a lesbian," says Saunders of Andrews. "But her mum and dad were middle class and snotty, so she told them I was a man to keep herself clear. I couldn't believe it when I was arrested. I went along with all the stupid things she was saying, as I loved her more than anything else in the world."

In sentencing Saunders in the Yorkshire court, Judge James Crabtree explained that she was being harshly punished as a deterrent to other lesbians. "You have called into account their whole sexual identity, and I suspect both girls would rather have been raped by some young man than have happen to them what you did," Crabtree said to Saunders. "In these days of sexual openness about lesbianism and bisexual behavior, I think I have to ensure that anybody else who is tempted to try and copy what you did will count the cost of it."

"She was given a very, very long sentence for someone just sixteen at the time," says Fulford. "For a judge to claim that these women would rather be raped by a man than have consenting sex with another woman is, frankly, outrageous."

During the appeal hearing, Fulford asked the court to consider Saunders's "exceptional background and disturbed childhood, including sexual abuse." He also cited the report of a prison social worker who described Saunders as a model prisoner and recommended that she be freed and given "the proper counseling, assistance, and advice." In granting Saunders's release, appeals judge Lord Justice Staughton cited the prison report, Saunders's youth, and his own doubts that her severe sentence would act as a deterrent to other lesbians.

After the judge announced his decision, Saunders was whisked off to a celebration by her supporters who had filled the courtroom. For months Saunders's case has provided lesbian London with a truly queer hero. Members of a group called LABIA — Lesbians Answer Back in Anger — have demonstrated for her release and written to her in prison.

Over a drink, Saunders told her supporters that her time in Styal Prison had not been all bad. "The prison's full of dykes," she said. "I've had a girlfriend for nine months. It's like Paradise City in Styal. They all kept joking about my dildo." But, she disclosed, "there never was no dildo. They thought there had to be a penis involved, so they said that about the dildo." She paused and grinned. "My tongue was good enough."

I Don't think you know what BUTCH IS...

©1992 by Di Massa

SOME GIRLS THINK IT'S BUTCH TO SPIT REAL FAR.

TOOOEY

SPLAT

TAKE DAT!

OR to find that 'just right' pair of LEVIS that HIDES amy HIPS

if I stand jes right it even bulges!

Some girls do butchy by being seen with a cigarette hanging out of their mouth!

HUH? WHO, ME?

d'ya get the picture?

yes, we see!

or to have greasy, dirty car hands!

KIN YA FIXIT?

· · · ?

OR TO TIE UP, CLAMP, SLICE, CUT, WHIP, ASS-FUCK, BURN, GAG AND ENEMA THEIR GIRLFRIEND!!

the lil' DICKENS

she LOVES it!!

DADDY

BUT THEY'RE ALL CARTOONS COMPARED TO RANDY RAE.

RANDY RAE LIVES ON A FARM, SHE'S 17, AND SHE'S NEVER SEEN A GAY PUBLICATION

MATTER O'FACT, SHE'S NEVER BEEN OUT OF SCRATCHANKLE, MISSISSIPPI. SHE LIVES WITH HER MA AND CUTS WOOD AND DOES OTHER FARM THINGS.

HER HANDS ARE DIRTY AND CALLOUSED, SHE CAN'T READ, AND SHE AIN'T NEVER HEARD OF NO DOC MARTEN.

RANDY RAE'S CLOTHES FIT IN ONE DRAWER. BESIDES THAT SHE OWNS A SILVER CIGARETTE LIGHTER AND A RIFLE.

NOBODY THINKS SHE'S UNNATURAL. HER MA LOVES HER, SAYS:" SHE'S JES' RANDY RAE, ALWAYS BEEN THIS WAY"

"DOES ALL THE WORK 'ROUN HERE, GITS UP AT 5:00 AM, TENDS THIS WHOLE DANG FARM, COMES IN THE HOUSE AND EATS LIKE A HORSE"

"GITS HER BUILD FROM HER DADDY, AN' SHE KIN FIX DAMN NAR INNYTHANG THET KIN GIT BROKE!"

"THERE AIN'T A LOTTA FOLKS THO, MOST OF THEM'S RELATIVES ANYWAY. RECKON SHE'S CLOSEST TO HER ANT DELORES."

"ON SATURDEE NAHTS THEY GITS IN ALL KINE-SA TRUBBLE!"

"GOES OUT A-HOOTIN' AN' A HOLLERIN' AN' LORD ONLY KNOWS WHAT!"

"DON'T SEE NEITHER-A THEIR HIDES TIL SUPPERTIME ON SUNDAY!!"

DIANE DIMASSA

SHE DON'T DATE, AND NONE OF THE LOCAL BOYS BOTHER HER AFTER WHAT SHE DID TO THAT LENNY FELLA

RANDY RAE'S LIFE WAS ONE HARD-WORKIN' DAY AFTER ANOTHER. SHE WAS SIMPLE, UNSPOILED, + CONTENT

ONE DAY COUSIN JUNE WANDERED OVER AND STARTED HANGIN' AROUND.

JUNE WAS 15, AND HAD WHAT YOU WOULD CALL A REPUTATION.

SHE'D SET UP THERE ON THAT PORCH AND SPY RANDY RAE ALL DAY LONG.

AT NIGHT SHE ACTED LIKE SHE COULDN'T HELP HERSELF, SLOBBERIN' AN' CLIMBIN' AN' A FLIRTIN'

SHE NEVER WAS MUCH FOR SELF-CONTROL AND COULD BARELY STAND BEIN' AROUND RANDY RAE ANYWAY. ONE NIGHT SHE SAID:

RANDY RAE OBLIGED.

THEY WENT OFF QUICK TO THE BARN. RANDY RAE NEVER DONE IT BEFORE BUT SHE FIGURED SHE WAS GOOD WITH HER HANDS, SO...

JUNE MADE SOUNDS SHE NEVER HEARD HERSELF MAKE BEFORE.

THEY DID IT EVERYWHERE CONSTANTLY. JUNE MADE A DECISION.

SHE SAID: "RANDY RAE, YOU MAKE MAH HART BEAT LIKE NONE OTHER. YOU BEST RUN AN' TELL YER MAMA THAT AH INTENDS TO MARRY YOU."

DIANE DIMASSA

AND MARRY THEY DID. AND THE JP WAS NONE OTHER THAN ANT DELORES, WHO WAS TICKLED PINK!

MAMA TRIED NOT TO SHOW IT, BUT SHE LOVED HAVIN' JUNE AROUND. JUNE LOVED HER JUST CAUSE SHE WAS RANDY RAE'S MAMA.

THEY WAS HAPPY AND THEY STAYED HAPPY. SOON LITTLE ONES STARTED SHOWIN' UP

NOBODY NEVER ASKED NO QUESTIONS. JUNE' RANDY RAE HAD 11 KIDS, AND MOST FOLKS SAID THEY WERE ON ACCOUNT OF JUNE'S RUNNIN' AROUND.

BUT THE REAL TRUTH WAS THEY DIDN'T KNOW **WHAT** TO BELIEVE, BECAUSE THERE WAS ONE OBVIOUS FACT THAT COULD NOT BE DENIED BY NO ONE...

AND THAT WAS THAT EVERY SINGLE ONE-A THEM ELEVEN KIDS LOOKED 'ZACKLY LIKE RANDY RAE!

AND THAT IS THE FINAL WORD IN **BUTCH**

Butch Icons of the Silver Screen

JENNI OLSON

WHEN I was little, I could recognize myself in the faces and screen characters of Tatum O'Neal, Jodie Foster, and Kristy McNichol. These little tomboys empowered me to think of myself as a hero. They were strong and smart like the movie cowboys and gangsters I emulated. They were "different," and that difference was celebrated on screen as good old-fashioned individuality.

On screen, tomboys were socially acceptable. As a young butch dyke coming out in 1986, I looked for their grown-up counterparts. I couldn't find anything. My trio of tomboy heroes hadn't turned out like I had. Instead, I turned to Marlon Brando and James Dean as my role models of butchness.

Then, when I was a twenty-three-year-old film studies major at the University of Minnesota, Vito Russo's book *The Celluloid Closet* opened the door to a vast world of lesbian and gay film images — a new landscape of culture, heroes, and recognition. I don't remember how I got my hands on it, but I do remember that I couldn't put it down.

I wanted to see the films Vito wrote about. Not just on video in the privacy of my own home, but with an audience full of people who wanted to see them as badly as I did. With lists of film titles in my head, I approached the student film committee with my proposal for "Lavender Images: A Lesbian and Gay Film Retrospective." Their unenthusiastic approval left me alone and uncertain in front of a shelf full of 16mm film distribution catalogs. Finding the source for

The Killing of Sister George after hours of searching, I began my career as a film programmer. I also began my own informal inventory (and source list) of butch women in film.

The films included here are all feature-length motion pictures, mostly Hollywood productions, some independently produced. Most of these films are available for rental on video. A brief list of mail order distributors specializing in lesbian and gay films on video is included along with listings of non-theatrical distributors for specific titles (in case you want to present your own Butch Film Festival). There are many interesting works dealing with gender issues and butchness being produced in short format film and video, and a brief listing of some of these films is also included.

TOMBOY

• Robin Johnson. *Times Square*; Allan Moyle, USA (1980). Robin Johnson's cocky streetwise Nicky is one of the sweetest dyke portrayals ever. She's tough and romantic, shy and insecure; she's a hero, she's a gravel-voiced, tough talking, rock 'n' roll icon. She does the butch/femme thing with Pammy (Trini Alvarado) as they play off each other's strengths and insecurities like the classic lesbian couple. "I'm brave, but you're pretty. I'm a fuckin' freak of nature," she tells Pammy. While there's no explicit lesbian content in the film, the original script had several scenes and plot elements that developed the sexual butch/femme tension between Nicky and Pammy, including: their first meeting in the hospital in which they have to undress in front of each other; two scenes where they take off their shirts and play together in their underwear in the river; a wrestling scene; the first night that they sleep (sleep, not fuck) together; and a scene where Pammy dances topless at the Cleo Club while Nicky watches. Despite all this missing content, there's tons of erotic tension between the girls, and, most importantly, they love each other, and they're not interested in boys.

Also see:

• Little Jodie Foster in everything she was in before she grew up and her voice changed — especially Gary Nelson's *Freaky Friday*, USA (1976) and Nicolas Gessner's *The Little Girl Who Lives Down the Lane*, USA (1976).

• Little Tatum O'Neal in Peter Bogdanovich's *Paper Moon*, USA (1973), Michael Ritchie's *Bad News Bears,* USA (1976), and Ronald F. Maxwell's *Little Darlings,* USA (1980). She's not actually all that butch in *Little Darlings,* but she's very cute, and it's such a great movie. She and Kristy McNichol and the other girls are all so in love with each other that you can read it as an allegory of closeted lesbian adolescence. Kristy McNichol, of course, is the butch one. As Kristy and Tatum race to lose their virginity, Kristy's the one who sleeps with a boy – and you know it's really to prove that she's not a dyke. But you know that she *is* a dyke – which makes it a really moving film. I saw this in a theatre when I was seventeen and I identified on an intensely uncomfortable level with Kristy McNichol. It was a very strange experience to see my awkward tomboy self in a Hollywood movie. And Kristy probably wasn't acting; she was just being herself as the uncomfortable-in-her-body, Marlboro-smoking, teenage butch with the jean jacket and bad '70s adolescent girl haircut.

• Mary Stuart Masterson in Howard Deutch's *Some Kind of Wonderful,* USA (1987). She gets dirty, she plays drums, she pretends she's interested in Eric Stultz, but she doesn't actually do anything about it. There's all kinds of coded dialogue about her being "different" from other girls. And she's totally cute. Way better than her Annie Hall-butch Idgy in *Fried Green Tomatoes.*

• Mercedes McCambridge (in a small, uncredited part) as the dykey Chicana juvenile delinquent in Orson Welles's *Touch of Evil,* USA (1958). When the boys ask the girls to leave the room as they prepare to gang-rape Janet Leigh, McCambridge insists, "I wanna watch."

• Julie Harris as Frankie in Fred Zinneman's *Member of the Wedding,* USA (1953).

FTM (Women as Men/Girls as Boys)

• Tomoko Otakra, Rie Mizuhara, Miyuki Nakano, and Eri Miyagima. *Summer Vacation: 1999;* Shusuke Kaneko, Japan (1988). *Summer Vacation* looks at the shifting attractions between four boys at an isolated country school. Vivid character development, clever narrative structure and a striking visual atmosphere come together in this beautiful cinematic fantasy. In a brilliant genderbending casting twist, director Kaneko cast girls in the male roles, later dubbing in their voices with those of four male actors. While most Western audiences are familiar

TIMES SQUARE

SUMMER VACATION

with the *Noh/Kabuki* tradition of Japanese theater in which female roles are played by men, *Summer Vacation* draws on the less well-known *Takurazuka* tradition, in which male roles are played by women.

• Pamela Segall. *Something Special*; Paul Schneider, USA (1985). In this obscure teen transgender comedy, Milly Niceman wishes she were a boy and then wakes in the middle of the night to discover she's magically grown "a guy's thing down there." Her family and friends make the adjustment to her new male self, Willy, and the film plays extensively on all of the homo- and lesbo-erotic potentials available. She goes back to being a girl at the end (so she can be with a boy), but she's still a butch girl even if she is straight.

• Anne Carlisle. *Liquid Sky*; Slava Tsukerman, USA (1983). Anne Carlisle's performance as queer twin brother and sister is one of the sexiest examples of androgyny ever filmed. As original as they come, this sci-fi sex-and-drug story is raw, funny, and strangely moving. (I fell in love with Anne Carlisle after seeing this film and ran to the video store to find anything else she was in; the only thing I could find was a really boring drama in which she looks and acts completely normal. Resist the temptation to rent it — I can't even remember its name — just watch *Liquid Sky* again.)

• Marta Keler. *Virgina*; Srdjan Karanovic, Yugoslavia/France (1991). *Virgina* offers a remarkable look at the workings of misogyny, gender, and sex roles in nineteenth-century Serbia. The film's title is taken from the Serbian term used to describe a girl raised as a boy. This practice seems to have been not entirely uncommon; according to superstition, lack of a son would bring about the family's demise. Born as the fourth daughter of a poor Serbian family, "Stephen" narrowly escapes being shot at birth by her father. Raised as a boy, Stephen sees her mother and sisters treated abusively by her father. Her empathy for them as a woman is countered by her family's insistence that she indulge her own male privilege. Her mother consoles her, "Better a rooster for a day than a hen for life. Everything is made for men." Growing up to be a handsome young boy, Stephen finds a boyfriend and a girlfriend, and a good deal of erotic tension with both. A tragedy provokes Stephen's eventual rebellion against her father, and in a surprising revelation, Stephen's masquerade is shown to be a common thread in the fabric of this androcentric Serbian culture. The film was completed during the outbreak of the civil war in June 1991.

Also see:

• Eva Mattes. *A Man Like Eva*; Radu Gabrea, Germany (1983). Eva Mattes stars as Rainer Werner Fassbinder in this rather slow fictionalized portrayal of the late great gay director.

FTMTF (Women as Men Who Become Women)

• Vanessa Redgrave. *Second Serve*; Anthony Page, USA (1986). Redgrave is so convincing as a man in the first part of this made-for-television bio-pic of tennis coach Renée Richards that it's hard to believe she's a woman in the second part.

Also see:

• Anne Heywood as Roy/Wendy in John Dexter's *I Want What I Want*, USA (1972). Heywood (*The Fox*) is totally weird (not really butch, but very queer) in this bizarre sex-change melodrama. The film ultimately comes across as a plea for transsexual understanding as Roy becomes Wendy and falls in love with a man. A camp gem with much unintentional humor. Watch for the period styles in home furnishings, hair, clothing, and especially makeup.

• Micheline Carvel in *Adam Is Eve*, France (1953).

Gender Dysphoria

• Ana Beatriz Nogueira. *Vera*; Sergio Toledo, Brazil (1986). Presenting the story of a young woman who believes that she is a man, *Vera* deals with issues of masculine/butch identification and internalized misogyny, and portrays the dysfunctional effects of rigid gender-role stratification. Vera does not identify herself as a lesbian (she believes she's a man in a woman's body). Vera grows up in an orphanage, and on being released when she turns eighteen, takes a job at a research center where she meets Clara, with whom she falls in love. Vera's insistence that she is a man becomes problematic when, in a painfully intimate love scene, she refuses to remove her undershirt. The relationship between Clara and Vera is seriously jeopardized as they both struggle with Vera's gender dysphoria. Two notes about the film: The film employs an unusually fluid, and at times hard to follow, flashback structure to show parts of Vera's life in the orphanage. An ambiguous ending (open to two very different interpretations) makes the film extremely disturbing.

ADAM IS EVE

Also see:

• Mink Stole in John Waters's *Desperate Living*, USA (1977). When her girlfriend says she doesn't like her sex change, she cuts off her cock with a scissors and throws it out the door.

GENERAL GENDERFUCK

• Shelley Mars. *The Virgin Machine*; Monika Treut, West Germany (1988). Shelley Mars does double-duty drag: as Ramona the sex therapist, she poses in the stylized lesbian fuck scene with Ina Blum; and as Martin the sleazy male chauvinist pig, she performs her famous Burlezk drag/strip routine. He strips down to his shirttails and boxer shorts, jacks off a beer bottle, and cums foam all over the stage.

• Ellen Barkin. *Switch*; Blake Edwards, USA (1992). A truly weird rendering of what could have been a predictable retread. Barkin as Amanda/Steve plays up the slapstick and sexism of masculinity and goes a bit over the top on the artifice of femininity. His/her budding feminist consciousness provides plenty of cathartic moments (à la *Thelma & Louise*), and there's homo/lesbo-eroticism everywhere. The ad campaign for *Switch* posed the genderfuck question of the year: "Will being a woman make him a better man?" There *was* an extensive girl/girl love scene between Ellen Barkin and Lorraine Bracco; unfortunately the scene was cut after test audiences responded negatively to it at pre-screenings of the film. In a cover story interview, "The Sexiest Man Alive," in *Entertainment Weekly*, Barkin said of the excised love scene: "There was no nudity or anything, but it was a lot heavier than what's in the film now. [Director] Blake [Edwards] didn't want to cut it. And to me it really elevated the film. But the audiences weren't ready for that. I felt that [Blake and the studio] should have just shoved it down their throats. It would have been a great thing for gay women." As Barkin describes the final version of the scene, it sounds a bit too much like what Stephen Spielberg did to the love scene between Celie and Shug in his "version" of *The Color Purple*. Barkin says, "Lorraine and I came up with this idea that my character would get the giggles and out of nerves have uncontrollable fits of laughter while Lorraine was very seriously trying to make love to her." Alas, another Hollywood lesbian love scene goes down (as it were) in history, right alongside the tickling scene in *Personal Best*. Who says lesbians don't have a sense of humor? Looking at Hollywood, it seems that's *all* we have. We certainly don't have sex.

• Carole Landis. *Turnabout*; Hal Roach, USA (1940). Husband and wife change bodies halfway through this screwball comedy. The comic talents of Carole Landis bring a measure of intelligence and hilarity to a fairly lightweight script. She dresses up in big man clothes and mimics male body language, speech, and gesture.

• Veronica Lake. *Sullivan's Travels*; Preston Sturges, USA (1941). The plot makes no use at all of Veronica Lake's boy-drag as she dresses up to go slumming with Joel McCrea. (As they walk through a shanty town holding hands, director Sturges seems oblivious to any notion of homo-eroticism.) The film's feel-good populism (à la Frank Capra) focuses on Joel McCrea as Everyman, and Lake is, of course, merely a woman. She steals the film from McCrea when she's on screen and (along with Bacall and Dietrich) has one of the sexiest deep voices ever heard – they call it sultry when femmes talk that way.

PASSING

• Katharine Hepburn. *Sylvia Scarlett*; George Cukor, USA (1936). Hepburn previously did a bit of crossdressing in Dorothy Arzner's 1933 woman-aviator melodrama, *Christopher Strong*. Here she goes all out as Sylvester Scarlett, boy thief and traveling musician. It's a crazy plot that veers bizarrely from comedy to tragedy. As with Garbo's *Queen Christina*, the latter half of the film is disappointing. But Hepburn's a bundle of boy energy, looks like a young David Bowie, and even has a girl kiss her on the lips.

• Greta Garbo. *Queen Christina*; Rouben Mamoulian, USA (1933). The one and only Garbo gives the drag performance of her career as the titular seventeenth-century queen. Swaggering about castle and countryside in male attire, the Swedish queen is as butch as they come and then some. Although the real life queen was a lesbian, the film has her falling in love with John Gilbert. Just underneath the heterosexual act, however, is a clear queer appeal, and it's easy to imagine the queen as a dyke. Christina's apparent love interest through the first half of the film is the Countess Ebba Sparre (Elizabeth Young), and an early scene in the film features a very nice butch/femme sort of kiss between the two.

JENNI OLSON

SYLVIA SCARLETT

When Christina meets Antonio (John Gilbert) in a country inn (where she is traveling in male disguise), they end up having to share a room together. In a very provocative sequence of misgendered identities, the queen is propositioned by a barmaid. She reveals to Antonio that she is a woman, and, on waking in bed together the following morning, the couple is seen by a servant who raises his eyebrows at the two "men."

When pressed by her valet to marry ("But, your majesty, you cannot die an old maid"), the queen replies, "I have no intention to ... I shall die a bachelor."

Indeed, Garbo herself died a bachelor, and at this point her own lesbianism is common knowledge. The behind-the-scenes history of this film (according to Mercedes D'Acosta's autobiography) is that Garbo and D'Acosta, who had been lovers, developed the film together. Later D'Acosta was fired as screenwriter from the project because she was making it too clear that the queen was a lesbian. This seems to come through quite clearly in the beginning of the film, and changes somewhat strangely when the queen has a fight with the Countess somewhere in the second reel. The queen thereafter toys with the affections of a court ambassador (who obviously does not interest her) until she meets Antonio. When she gives up her throne to be with Antonio (in real life she gave it up to be with Ebba Sparre) the film makes its ultimate break with reality.

In *The Celluloid Closet*, Vito Russo cites the following excerpt from a 1933 *New York Herald-Tribune* book review which makes reference to the anticipated release of the film: "The one persistent love of Christina's life was for the Countess Ebba Sparre, a beautiful Swedish noblewoman who lost most of her interest in Christina when Christina ceased to rule Sweden ... the evidence is overwhelming, but will Miss Garbo play such a Christina?" Unfortunately no. Small consolation — Antonio dies and Christina goes off alone in the end.

Also see:

• Julie Andrews in Blake Edwards's *Victor/Victoria*, USA (1982). Remember *The Sound of Music*? Julie Andrews doesn't really seem very convincing as a man, does she?

• Barbra Streisand in her own *Yentl*, USA (1983). Another Barbra Streisand movie I didn't see.

• Molly Picon in Joseph Green's *Yiddle with His Fiddle*, Poland (1937). A movie Barbra Streisand saw before she made *Yentl*.

Cowboy Butch

• Anne Bancroft. *Seven Women*; John Ford, USA (1966). Bancroft struts her stuff as the chain-smoking, cowboy crossdressing Dr. Cartwright. She's tough, bold, intelligent and doesn't take shit from anyone (until the end, when she is forced — albeit heroically — into a submissive role). The film also features Margaret Leighton as Agatha Andrews, the repressed lesbian spinster with the hots for Sue Lyon. Set in 1935 China, in an all-women mission, *Seven Women* is remarkable for offering an intense psychological study of its female characters. Unfortunately, the portrayal of the film's Mongolian robbers is not so enlightened, falling into the usual Hollywood racist stereotypes in the last half of the picture.

• Joan Crawford and Mercedes McCambridge. *Johnny Guitar*; Nicholas Ray, USA (1954). More cowboy drag, and good feudin' between Joan and Mercedes.

Also see:

• Betty Hutton in 501s and facial hair in the "Oh Them Dudes" production number in *Let's Dance*, USA (1950); Beverly Garland in Roger Corman's *Gunslinger*, USA (1956); Jane Russell in *Montana Belle*, USA (1952); Doris Day in *Calamity Jane*, USA (1953); Louise Dresser in *Caught*, USA (1931); Martha Sleeper in *West of the Pecos*, USA (1934); Barbara Hale in *West of the Pecos*, USA (1945); and Dorothy Gish in *Nugget Nell*, USA (1919).

• Last but not least, check out Suzi Quatro as Leather Tuscadero on TV's "Happy Days."

Law Enforcement

• Jodie Foster. *Silence of the Lambs*; Jonathan Demme, USA (1991). She has the sexiest butch hands.

• Jamie Lee Curtis. *Blue Steel*; Kathryn Bigelow, USA (1990). A stupid ending (her sleeping with the big he-man cop), but who can resist a girl with a gun?

Also see:

• Hope Emerson in her Academy Award nominated portrayal of the sadistic prison matron Evelyn Harper in John Cromwell's *Caged*, USA (1950). Also Eleanor Parker in the last half of the film (after she gets her head shaved).

Strong Female Characters Who Look Really Butch When They're All Sweaty and Dirty

• Sigourney Weaver and Jenette Goldstein. *Aliens*; Ridley Scott, USA (1986). Sigourney's hot, but hotter still is Jenette Goldstein as Private Vasquez. When one of the male cadets hassles her about her butchness, asking: "Have you ever been mistaken for a man?" She simply responds, "No, have you?"

• Linda Hamilton in *Terminator 2*; James Cameron, USA (1992).

"So, Which One of You Is the Man?" Butch Lesbians in Mainstream Lesbian-Relationship Films

• Patrice Donnelly. *Personal Best*; Robert Towne, USA (1982). The lesbianism of Mariel (femme) Hemingway's character is treated as a phase (she goes off with a male water-polo player in the end). Patrice Donnelly's character is the "real" lesbian — basic butch. Good butch dialogue. In response to Hemingway's reluctance to define the true nature of their relationship, Donnelly says, "We may be friends, but we also happen to fuck each other every once in a while." And (on meeting Hemingway's new boyfriend): "He's pretty cute... for a guy." A memorable love scene, consisting of tickling and nervous giggling and Mariel Hemingway saying, "This isn't so bad, I kind of like this."

• Jane Hallaren in John Sayles's *Lianna*, USA (1983). Barely butch.

• Beryl Reid in Robert Aldrich's *The Killing of Sister George*, England (1968). Late '60s British butch.

• Anne Heywood in Mark Rydell's *The Fox,* USA (1968). Femmey-butch. Very sexy in and out of her hunting outfit. A truly awful film.

Butch Lesbians in Independent Lesbian-Themed Films

• Patricia Charbonneau. *Desert Hearts*; Donna Deitch, USA (1986). Sort of butch, butchier than Helen Shaver. Good butch dialogue: "Take your hands out of your pockets and come here."

• Sheila Dabney. *She Must Be Seeing Things*; Sheila McLaughlin,

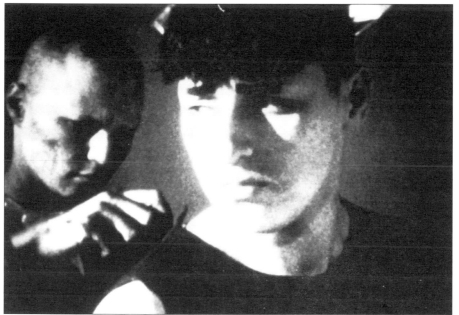

FLAMING EARS

STORME DELARVERIE

JENNI OLSON

USA (1987). Overly ambitious at times, this feature is notable for its treatment of the explicitly butch/femme relationship between Agatha and Jo.

• Linda Basset. *Waiting for the Moon*; Jill Godmilow USA (1987). Basset plays butch Gertrude Stein opposite Linda Hunt's brilliant Alice B. Toklas.

Also see:

• k.d. lang in *Salmonberries*; Percy Adlon, Germany (1992). *Salmonberries* portrays the developing emotional bonds between two women of very different backgrounds. Roswitha (Rosel Zech), a librarian in the small Alaskan mining town of Kotzebue, resists lang's affections throughout the film. lang's determined courting climaxes in a tremendous tease of a love scene (or, not a love scene). lang's abilities as an actress are difficult to determine. She doesn't talk much, and she's so captivating when she's on screen that it's hard to care whether she can act or is just being herself. Whichever, she gives a hot cinematic rendering of a strong, silent butch dyke in love.

CYBERDYKE (POSTMODERN BUTCH)

• Angela Hans Scheirl. *Flaming Ears*; Angela Hans Scheirl, Dietmar Schipek and Ursula Purrer, Austria (1992). As the sullen necrophiliac cyborg, Scheirl wanders the streets reciting some of the most poetically romantic (butch loner) monologues ever written. She's tall, lean, dirty and handsome in her red PVC coveralls. The sweet tenderness in her puppy-like devotion to her new lover's corpse is an inspiring piece of postmodern butch.

BUTCH BEHIND THE CAMERA

• Dorothy Arzner, openly lesbian Hollywood director of the 1930s. In October, 1936 *Time* magazine described her as "short, stocky, with a quiet executive manner, a boyish bob and an interest in medicine and sunsets." Her unique sensibility shines through in such classics as *Christopher Strong* (1933), *Craig's Wife* (1936), and *Dance, Girl, Dance* (1940).

A Sampling of Contemporary Short Films and Videos Dealing with Butchness, Gender Identity, Masculinity and Female-to-Male Transgender Issues

• *Brown Sugar Licks Snow White*; Suzi Silbar and Robin Vachal, USA (1992), 4 mins B&W. [video source: Video Data Bank] Snippets of voice, text, and image scan the terrain of race and gender, with porno dialogue and girls in femme drag.

• *Dual of the Senses*; Heidi Arnesen, USA (1991), 3 mins. B&W [16mm source: Frameline] Girl dresses up as boy to do it with boy dressed up as girl.

• *F2M*; Cayte Latta, Australia (1992), 15 mins. [video source: Australian Film Commission] Interview with Jasper, a thirty-year-old lesbian female-to-male pre-op transsexual.

• *It Wasn't Love*; Sadie Benning, USA (1992), 20 mins. [video source: Video Data Bank] Sadie does her Fats Domino impression, sucks her thumb, tells a story about her girlie, and smiles sweet for the camera.

• *Juggling Gender*; Tami Gold, USA (1992), 27 mins. [video source: Women Make Movies] A lesbian performance artist talks about growing up, coming out, lesbian feminism, and having a beard.

• *Linda/Les and Annie*; Annie Sprinkle, Al Jacoma, Johnny Armstrong, USA (1989), 28 mins. [video source: Annie Sprinkle] Transsexual Les Nichols and Annie Sprinkle talk about Les's operation and life, and then fuck with Les's prosthesis.

• *Max*; Monika Treut, USA/Germany (1992), 20 mins. [16mm source: First Run Features] Female-to-male transsexual Max Valerio talks about his life and the experience of becoming a man.

• *Passing*; Sara Whiteley, USA (1991), 3 mins. 16mm B&W. [16mm source: Frameline]. A woman is made over to a masculine and then a feminine extreme.

• *P[l]ain Truth*; Ilppo Pohjola, Finland (1993), 15 mins. [35mm source: Zeitgeist Films] A painful and cathartic "symbolic documentary" based on the experience of Rudi, a female-to-male transsexual.

• *Stafford's Story*; Susan Muska, USA (1992), 3 mins. [video source: Frameline]. Stafford tells about an encounter at a sex club.

• *Storme: The Lady of the Jewel Box*; Michelle Parkerson, USA (1987), 21 mins. [16mm source: Women Make Movies]. An overview of the career of the famous black male-impersonator, Storme DeLarverie.

INDEX OF FEATURE TITLES [WITH SOURCES]:

Aliens [Films Inc.]
Blue Steel [Swank]
Calamity Jane [Kit Parker Films]
Desert Hearts [Samuel Goldwyn]
Desperate Living [Films Inc.]
Flaming Ears [Women Make Movies]
The Fox [Films Inc.]
The Killing of Sister George [Films Inc.]
Lianna [Swank]
Liquid Sky [New Yorker]
A Man Like Eva [New Yorker]
Personal Best [Swank]
Queen Christina [Swank]
Seven Women [Films Inc.]
She Must Be Seeing Things [First Run Features]
Silence of the Lambs [Swank]
Something Special [Cori International]
Some Kind of Wonderful [Films Inc.]
Sullivan's Travels [Swank]
Summer Vacation: 1999 [New Yorker]
Switch [Swank]
Times Square [Swank]
Touch of Evil [Swank]
Turnabout [Budget]
Vera [Kino International]
Victor/Victoria [Swank]
Virgina [Mercure Distribution]
Virgin Machine [First Run Features]
Waiting for the Moon [Samuel Goldwyn]
Yentl [Swank]
Yiddle with His Fiddle [Em Gee Film Library/Brandeis University]

FILM AND VIDEO EXHIBITION SOURCES:

Australian Film Commission, 61 2 925-7333
Brandeis University — National Center for Jewish Film,
    (617) 899-7044

Cori International, 2049 Century Park East, #780, Los Angeles, CA
90067 (310) 557-0173

Em Gee Film Library, 6924 Canby Avenue, Suite 102, Reseda, CA
91335 (818) 981-5506

Films Inc., 5547 N. Ravenswood Avenue, Chicago, IL 60640
(800) 323-4222, Ext. 42

First Run Features, 153 Waverly Place, New York, NY 10014
(212) 243-0600

Frameline, 346 Ninth St., San Francisco, CA 94103 (415) 703-8650

Kino International, 333 W 39th Street, Suite 503, New York, NY
10018 (212) 629-6880

Kit Parker Films, 1245 Tenth Street, Monterey, CA 93940
(800) 538-5838

Mercure Distribution, FAX (33-1) 45-65-07-47

New Yorker Films, 16 W 61st Street, New York, NY 10023
(212) 247-6110

Samuel Goldwyn Co., 10203 Santa Monice Boulevard #500,
Los Angeles, CA 90067 (310) 552-2255

Annie Sprinkle, P.O. Box 1024, Long Island City, NY 11101

Swank, 201 S. Jefferson/P.O. Box 231, St. Louis, MO 63166
(800) 876-5577

Tara Releasing, 124 Belvedere #5, San Rafael, CA 94901
(415) 454-5838

Video Data Bank, 32 S Wabash Avenue, Chicago, IL 60603
(312) 899-5172

Women Make Movies, 225 Lafayette Street #206, New York, NY
10012 (212) 925-0606

Zeitgeist Films, 200 Waverly Place #4, New York, NY 10014
(212) 727-1989

CONTACT SOURCES FOR VIDEO RENTAL AND PURCHASE:

Charis Video, P.O. Box 797, Brooklyn, NY 11231

Facets Multimedia, 1517 W Fullerton Avenue, Chicago, IL 60614
(800) 331-6197

Lambda Rising, 1625 Connecticut Avenue NW, Washington DC
20009 (202) 462-6969

TLA Video, 332 South Street, Philadelphia, PA 19147
(215) 922-1014

Peppermint Patty and Her Sisters

Sometimes Others Called Them Sir

JOAN HILTY

ARE you still pissed that Thelma drove off that cliff? Are you tired of cheering on tough-talking, gun-toting babes who throw it all away for a man in the last reel? That movie dykes always wind up dead or wounded? Or that TV dykes have to be the femmiest creatures on God's green earth to keep the advertisers from having a stroke?

Try comics. They don't solve everything — I'll tell you that up front. But they had the market cornered on butchy women long before Sigourney picked up an M-16. Comics specialize in true fantasy, the creation of a limitless universe where women really can be eight feet tall, fly in outer space, blow up buildings, and never have menstrual cramps. Also, comics depend on continuity. A comic feature or book title needs a lot of primary characters to keep it going for years and years. That's the kind of job security women can't always find. Our comic sisters don't always have to have a man. These factors lay the groundwork nicely for sexual subversion.

Obviously, this is not a foolproof generalization. Comics can be just as cynically and brutally sexist as anything else. Much of the medium reflects men's fear of strong, independent women. That true-fantasy advantage has also allowed comics to contribute some of the gruesomest, cloddiest fuck-'n'-kill violence against women ever. And, true, most of the comic characters billed as feminist role models and tough-girl icons are still, beneath it all, heterosexual fashion plates with standard comic-book physiques.

Nevertheless, there's still a truck load of fabulous butch women out there waiting for us to follow their boot prints into a half-century's worth of comics. They're armed; you'll love them when they're angry.

A History Lesson in Four Panels

Up until the 1930s, cartoon women were a pretty femmey bunch, plugging along as harmless little girls, languid flappers and rescuable appendages to heroes. This began to change most noticeably with the 1934 introduction of Milton Caniff's *Terry and the Pirates,* a classic adventure buddy-boy strip. In his book *The Comics,* author and cartoonist Colton Waugh notes that "the first signs of the strip's unique quality were the Caniff women, from the start a new and fascinating breed... [They] expressed a fact somewhat suppressed in strips at that time: [B]ad women can be beautiful."

The Caniff women were lasciviously drawn, all right. But they were also strong, aggressive and independent as women had rarely been before. Caniff's most famous villain, the Dragon Lady, was a cold-blooded pirate and gang commander who wielded her pistol as adeptly as her cigarette holder. It's no coincidence that Caniff was one of the few to protest — making an angry speech, actually — when the National Cartoonist Society refused membership to cartoonist Hilda Terry on gender grounds in 1951.

The villainnesses of Chester Gould's *Dick Tracy* were an even tougher bunch. Pundits of the '30s and '40s deplored the detective strip's brutal urban realism. They may have been especially upset about characters like Mamma Trohs, a linebacker-sized gangster's moll who not only threw cops through plate-glass windows but wasn't above scalding her lover to death when he tried to ditch her. Mamma could have easily arm wrestled Dick for Tess Trueheart and won.

But the real jumping-off point came around 1940. The combined effect of *Superman* and World War II created a major opportunity for estrogen in the comics. Comic book publishing became big business, and the war sent women into the work force — including the comic book industry — in record numbers. In a two-year period, three dynamic women made entrances with their own features and became extremely popular: the Amazon princess Wonder Woman, the Nazi-battling Miss Fury, and reporter-adventurer Brenda Starr. Significantly, the latter two were created by women — Tarpe Mills and Dale Messick.

Again, all three were conventionally svelte, feminine and straight. But now that the fair maidens were running their own shows, further subversion became possible. Say "butches in the Sunday funnies," and most people, if they can think of anybody, will think of Hank. She was a coworker of Brenda Starr's who appeared to have fallen right out of a Joan Nestle book, tailored suits and all. She was so butch that the average casual reader could mistake her for male — which, given the mores of the times, might have been Messick's intention.

Some truly tough gals showed up in the newspaper strip *Dickie Dare* when its creator, the aforementioned Colton Waugh, turned it over to his wife, Mabel Odin Burvik, in 1944. In one Sunday strip, men are chucked around like rag dolls by Hazie and Dazie, a formidable tag team of female bodyguards. In another, a little boy watches a steam shovel rumbling through a construction site, and is about to assume that its operator must be a "big, tough (man)" when the woman behind the wheel doffs her cap with a grin. He's speechless. She *is* big and tough. "I can't believe it! Why?" he gasps. "I was run down," she shrugs. "Needed to do lighter work."

Wartime also made possible the women — both two- and three-dimensional — of the Fiction House comic book company. As Trina Robbins and Cat Yronwode have documented in their 1985 *Women and the Comics,* Fiction House employed the most women artists and featured more female heroines than any of the numerous companies cranking out pulpy wartime adventure comics. The Fiction House protagonists were jungle princesses, gunfighters, and detectives, strong women in a male-dominated genre. Hearsay has it that at least two of the marvelous Fiction House artists — Frances Dietrick Hopper and Marcia Snyder — were gay. None of their characters was particularly butch, but Robbins and Yronwode deadpanned: "Hopper's renderings of women have a verve and sparkle often lacking in her drawings of men."

By creating strong, autonomous female characters that challenged sex roles, however slightly, these women creators were walking against a powerful cultural head wind. Consider the *Reefer Madness*-like tone of "That Strange Girl," a breathlessly paranoid story that ran in DC's romance comics line in the '60s. Baby butch Liz,

THAT STRANGE GIRL

JOAN HILTY

clad in lumberjack shirt and work boots, swaggers across the title page asking, "What was there about me that made me *different*? What set me apart from the *'normal'* girls? It pains me to tell this story, but if it can help ease the hurt in one girl who, like me, is torn by doubts and mixed emotions, it will be worth all the shame and torment I lived through when I was known as…THAT STRANGE GIRL." She's a tomboyish teenager who likes to help Dad with carpentry and yard work and — horrors! — prefers basketball to boys or clothes. "Some girls just don't *like* dresses," she tells her distraught mom, who snaps, "And some girls don't like *boys*, Liz!" Uh oh! She storms out and spends the night at her lov… um, friend Agnes's house. Agnes's mom says happily, "I *like* Agnes to have friends over. She's so *shy* with young people!"

"Agnes isn't shy once you get to *know* her," Liz grins, as Agnes reclines seductively in the background. By the way, these italics are all theirs, not mine. In the end, Liz falls safely for a boy, but the first four pages are priceless.

Later on in *Peanuts*, Charles Schultz introduced another classic baby butch, Peppermint Patty. Patty's adoring sidekick Marcy always called her "Sir," and a generation of little tomboys began to feel better about constantly winding up in the principal's office. She was eventually joined by Hank Ketchum's tall paisan playmate of Dennis the Menace, Gina, who always wore pants, knew how to fight, and disdained the usual little-girl stuff.

The myriad social upheavals of the previous decade created a big opening in the '70s, but only the underground comics responded. Mary Wings was the first to do lesbian autobiographical work, and dyke characters began to pop up in the work of well-known straight artists like S. Clay Wilson and Trina Robbins. The best butch babe, however, was to be found in *Dynamite Damsels*, Roberta Gregory's pioneering 1976 feminist comic book. Gregory's Doris was a rugged old-school butch with a bull tattoo on her chest, a lavender motorcycle, and great attitude. "We tough old dykes heal fast," she cracks, back on the job pumping gas after getting beaten up by gay-bashers.

To find the mainstream cartoon butch of the decade, however, you had to go to Japan. *The Rose of Versailles (Berusaiyu no Bara)* began as a serial in the weekly comic magazine *Margaret* in 1972. It ran to 1974 and seventeen hundred pages, and made its creator,

Riyoko Ikeda, Japan's most successful female cartoonist. It was a historically accurate drama based on the life of Marie Antoinette, but the real star was a swashbuckling babe, Oscar. As created by Ikeda, the fictional Oscar Françoise de Jarjayes is a woman raised as a man who becomes commander of the Versailles palace guard, and Marie's personal bodyguard. "Oscar's blurred sexuality allows her to take part in all the action and also to explore the thrills of love," writes Frederik Schodt in his 1988 book *Manga! Manga!* "In her flashy uniform, she drives both men and women to distraction." Granted, Oscar had the sparkly long-lashed eyes and petite measurements common to women in Japanese comics, but she sure looked hot in epaulets. Crossdressing heroines who become romantically (but never sexually) entangled with adoring femmes are a common theme in Japanese girls' comics.

But what happened to Hank and all those wild gals from the '40s? Back in the funny papers, things were looking grim for wild women. The end of World War II and a worsening economic climate for newspapers signaled the end of the large-format comic strip. The major action-adventure strips died out, and their slightly subversive, gun-totin' women went with them. *Brenda Starr* survives to this day, but Hank was married off in the '50s, probably at the urging of nervous editors.

After all, newspaper comics editors have always been a pretty conservative bunch, and over the past few decades they've favored simple, family-oriented, gag-a-day strips. By and large, cartoon women went back to being matriarchs, nagging wives of lovable main characters, and precocious little girls. Memo to a cartoonist: It's not too late to put Mary Worth on a Harley.

Super-Powers: A Great Way to Meet Chicks

Comic books have since won the tough-girl genre by default, but their track record as a whole has been spotty. Remember those handsome, stomping girls on your college sports teams who dated guys, made anxious fag jokes all the time, and then wound up bringing their girlfriends to your five-year reunion? They're alive and well all over the place at DC and Marvel Comics. They're gorgeous, tough, and in total denial. It's not really surprising. Not only are they hampered by the Comics Code, they're also created by straight men —

BRENDA STARR / THE CHICAGO TRIBUNE

HANK

SUICIDE SQUAD, DC COMICS

AMANDA WALLER

DYNAMITE DAMSELS, ROBERTA GREGORY

DORIS

ROGUE

who clearly like strong fantasy women, but only if they're still sexually available to them. It's no wonder they've got problems.

Marvel's *X-Men* is a particularly good example of this sort of weirdness. Although the series dwells heavily on the intolerance of "difference" — via the metaphor of hatred towards people with mutant powers — they've never featured an openly queer character.

Perhaps it's time they outed one. My choice would be Rogue, a former X-Men foe turned team member. It may just be my personal weakness for Southern butchy femmes ("Yo, Spiral — LATER!" she shouts at a foe she has been ordered to stop fighting), but ever since I encountered her in a skunk-striped bar-dyke haircut beating the crap out of Wolverine in her bad-guy days, I've pegged her for a closet case. Get this: Her mutant power consists in part of the ability to soak up people's psyches through skin contact, and she's permanently haunted by the fact that she absorbed the soul of superhero Ms. Marvel during a fight in San Francisco. Uh huh. Sounds like just another case of "clingus dykus" to me.

Another one of the title's butch babes is Yukio, a renegade samurai who prowls Tokyo's back streets at night looking for trouble. After meeting Yukio, X-Man Storm transforms from demure big-haired girl into mohawked babe in full leather. Obviously, those two did more than fight criminals in those back alleys. "Whatever it is — this madness of yours that has infected me — I welcome it," Storm announces.

And then there's Phoenix, a moody, crewcut fugitive from a nightmarish alternate future where mutants are hunted and killed under federal law. (When she escapes to 1984, she's already on the lam from a murderous demon-huntress, and darts into a nightclub. "Don't throw me out — she'll kill me!" she begs. "Who will?" the club owner asks. "Girlfriend, mos' likely," mutters the bouncer.)

In the present, Phoenix and the X-Man Kitty Pryde are platonic teammates, but they were definitely something else in that alternate future. Phoenix keeps looking at her dolefully, protecting her with junkyard-dog ferocity, and flashing back to their relationship in the alternate world. There, she tells us, Kitty was "part surrogate mother, mostly best friend." Yeah, sure.

Another one to look for is Amanda Waller, over in DC Comics. She's a butch black babe and the tailored commander of the Suicide Squad. She looks to be about 5'6" and two hundred fifty pounds — a physiological rarity among mainstream comic book butch women. And she delivers on the look: The cover of *Suicide Squad #10* features her shouting Batman into submission.

In another DC title, *Justice League International,* superheroes Mr. Miracle and Big Barda are a happily married couple. The only question is: Why? Miracle's a nice guy, but the attraction is lost on those of us who've seen the *very* strapping Barda battle the cosmic assassin Lobo, or just boss her teammates around like a dominatrix on Saturday night. Formerly a military officer on the planet Apokolips, she's marvelously broad-shouldered, buttheaded, and usually gets her way. JLI leader J'onn J'onnz is among the few who can boss Batman around, but when Barda's on the rampage he's reduced to constantly muttering, "I thought *I* was leader of this team."

Speaking of Batman, *The Dark Knight Returns,* a graphic novel that resurrected Batman as a crusty vigilante in a nightmarish future Gotham City, contributed another fine baby butch to the oeuvre. Handsomely drawn, *Dark Knight* was a smash when it came out in 1986, but it's insufferably hard-boiled, a black-and-blue testosterone fest. Luckily, this is alleviated by the presence of Carrie Kelley. She's a cute, sawed-off computer geek who barges into Batman's life uninvited as his new Robin. She lives the dream of baby dykes the world over: to blow your allowance on a good costume, sneak out via the fire escape, and spend the night beating up smelly boys — OK, homicidal mutant hoodlums.

JUSTICE LEAGUE INTERNATIONAL, DC COMICS

BIG BARDA

SUPERMAN, DC COMICS

MAGGIE SAWYER

JOAN HILTY

THE SENSATIONAL SHE-HULK

Ever since she was resurrected by John Byrne in 1989, I've wanted DC Comics's She-Hulk to come out. She's obviously drawn for the viewing pleasure of geeky comic book fanboys, but God, she's gorgeous. And buffed. And faintly tomboyish, and a major wiseass. And in the last pages of issue #1, she's definitely being cruised by a dykey cop who's watching her *get dressed.* ("Would it be OK for me to see the prisoners now?" says Shulkie, tucking in her shirttail. "Huh?" says the cop, distracted.) What's the hulkess waiting for? Hell, I'll chip in for the Doc Martens.

Besides, DC is statistically *the* hunting ground for genuine dykes. Whether their staff is more progressive or just more prurient is open to debate, but the fact remains that they've introduced several such characters in recent titles. There are the lovers Hazel and Foxglove in *Sandman,* and a distinctively dykey roommate in *Wonder Woman* #72, to name a few. But Byrne himself created the butchiest of them all when he was writing and drawing *Superman* in the '80s. He created Maggie Sawyer, police captain, lesbian mom, and lanky butch bombshell. In 1988, *Superman #15* even told her whole coming-out story, complete with a panel of Maggie getting cruised in a gay bar. But despite this Sapphic subplot and the fact that the main plot involves the daughter she lost custody of to her homophobic ex-husband, the script doesn't use the words "gay" or "lesbian" once.

You could protest that Maggie's penchant for miniskirts and cigarette holders is distinctly unbutch. But since she can plug a bat-winged demon with a .44 while plummeting through the air holding a screaming child, I'll let someone else argue the point with her.

SAVED BY THE INDIES

BUT THE real hotbeds of butchy babeness in the comics biz are the independents. These are the publications that have reaped the benefits of comics' long history of closeted dykedom — not to mention freedom from the Comics Code. *Love and Rockets,* for starters, by the prodigious Hernandez Brothers, has some truly marvelous women in its pages. Gilbert Hernandez's stories focus on the fictional town of Palomar, and two of its inhabitants are freckle-faced Riri and her busty, shit-kicking girlfriend, Maricela. How shit-kicking? Very. Nobody messes with Riri when her woman's around.

My favorite Hernandez brother, however, is Jaime, and he draws my favorite dykes. Maybe even my favorite women. Jaime has an artistic and narrative knack for strong, beautiful women that goes way beyond the usual prurient efforts of male comic artists. His most famous *Love and Rockets* characters, Maggie and Hopey, are a couple of best friends and sometimes lovers growing up in the Southern California barrio of Hoppers. In an early work, "Mechanix," Maggie is a top-flight mechanic whose work gets her mixed up with dictators, dinosaurs and revolution. Hopey is every good girl's dream and every school principal's nightmare: a baby butch hothead with a bass guitar and a high IQ. "I noticed you haven't been raising too much hell now that your lover Maggie's been gone," her brother taunts. "What's the matter, Casanova? Jealous because you can't get into her little panties?" Hopey grins. When he keeps it up, she attacks him with a staple gun. That's my girl.

But the real butch goddess babes in this drama are Maggie's aunt, pro wrestler Vicki Glori, and her former tag-team partner Queen Rena Titañon. They're both straight — although Rena's romantic history as of issue #41 remains tantalizingly unclear — but they're brass knuckle babes. Rena has been a world-champion wrestler, superhero, Queen of Zymbodia, and Black Fist Liberation Army guerrilla. Vicki, meanwhile, is a temperamental musclehead and fierce, conniving competitor with an indomitable will, going against her family's wishes

JOAN HILTY

LOVE AND ROCKETS, FANTAGRAPHICS

RENA TITAÑON

JEN CAMPER, GAY COMICS

BITCHY BUTCH

JOAN HILTY

and rising to the top of pro wrestling by reinventing herself as a gringa Texan named Cowgirl Vicki Lane. Jaime's narratives switch constantly between the past and the present, but whether they're eighteen or forty — in fact, especially when they're forty — Vicki and Rena are buffed, beautiful, completely self-made and unstoppable.

Tank Girl looks like Hopey's psycho twin sister and is the creation of Brits Jamie Hewlitt and Alan Martin. Distinguished by a violent temper and various stages of baldness, she storms through a high-energy, low-fashion world smokin' cigs and firin' a lot of assault weapons. She's popular among a lot of comics-reading women these days. That's not necessarily an endorsement. Granted, she's pretty hot and her rampages are mildly satisfying, but she lacks genuine womanly rage or the feminist smarts of Bitchy Bitch and Hothead Paisan. Basically, she's not much more than a homicidal boy with tits. It's that "violence-makes me horny" type of comic that looks great, but eventually makes the eyes glaze over.

Lest we forget the obvious, a new generation of queer cartoonists, inspired by decades of bad-girl comics and the women in their lives, draw a fine array of crazy butch women. Start with Alison Bechdel's Lois, the leather-jacketed Casanova of *Dykes to Watch Out For*. "If I waited three years between relationships," she muses, "I'd be... I'd be a hundred and two years old."

Move on to the work of Jennifer Camper, published in *On Our Backs, Gay Comix, Deneuve, Girljock* and a number of gay newspapers nationwide, whose sexy tough girls have been getting her in trouble with readers and publishers for years. Her idea of a new contingency group for future pride parades, as illustrated in *Gay Comix #17*, is "Big Mean Sweaty Dykes Just Looking For Trouble."

For a little leather, turn to the cartoon dykes of Terry Sapp (*The Adventures of Baby Dyke*) and Jacki Randall. And Fish's S/M-themed "One Fine San Francisco Evening" in *Real Girl #5* is a brass-knuckle antidote to what Roberta Gregory has called Twisted-Notions-Hetero-Males-Have-of-What-Women-Do-with-Each-Other alternative comix (in fact, Fish's title is almost a take-off on one of the better-known of these: *2 Girls on a Hot Summer Night*). Her rough sex scenes may not be your cup of tea, but the commanding presence of a sex comic created by dykes for dykes has value that can't be underestimated.

Gregory's own *Naughty Bits*, her solo comic from Fantagraphics, stars the crazed Bitchy Bitch and a host of li'l spinoff Bitchies, including, of course, Bitchy Butch — all flattop, black muscle tee and bad attitude. The Butch makes a guest appearance in *Gay Comix #17*, flipping out (to quote: "LIFE SUCKS THIS WORLD SUCKS PEOPLE SUCK HETEROS SUCK EVERYTHING SUCKS THIS CITY SUCKS THAT DOG SUCKS THIS STREET SUCKS....") and trying to cope with the sight of lipstick dykes and bisexual support groups ("Shit!... All I see is some teenager hooker rap group!!!"). Like Bitchy Bitch, Butch's anger is unfettered and politically incorrect.

Of course, no survey in this vein would be complete without the adventures of *Hothead Paisan: Homicidal Lesbian Terrorist*, who is, says creator Diane DiMassa in issue #5, "my own personal maniac, my enraged, lucid, passionate, plutonian playmate." Too much coffee and TV, with its barrage of woman-hating sex, violence and disinformation, regularly sends Hothead over the edge. She carves a machine-gun swath through the streets of her rough-edged East Coast city. Her targets range from tube-tying doctors to what a friend of mine calls "momos" — those guys who drive by you on the street and yell some kind of misogynistic shit out the window at you, but all you can hear is "momomsusudujsajkdhuh." Anyway, the book is funny as hell, and never self-righteous — Hothead's the first to admit she's a little unfocused. "I know the lesson by heart!" she shrieks at God during a dream in #4. "Life sucks an' then ya die!"

"Not only is that wrong," says God, "but we voted it Most Asinine Slogan Of All Time."

Hothead, Peppermint Patty, and their butch buddies in the funnies may just be able to link arms and march comics into the next century. Help them out by storming your local comics shop and acting out the law of supply and demand. It's fun to frighten the male customers who stand at the racks getting off on *Heavy Metal* and jumping when they see a woman, and if you know what to look for, the reading ain't bad either.

Many thanks to Julie Franki and Hope Barrett, and to Trina Robbins, author of the landmark A Century of Women Cartoonists.

Who Says There's Only Two Genders?

An Interview with JoAnn Loulan

ROXXIE

JoAnn *Loulan is a psychotherapist and author living in Northern California. She's written extensively on the subject of lesbian mental health and lesbian relationships, and is a dynamic and humorous speaker. Her books include* Lesbian Sex *and* Lesbian Passion *(Spinsters Ink). In this discussion, Roxxie and JoAnn Loulan counter the conventional answers to the question, Why Butch?*

JoAnn Loulan: I like the attitude of butches. I often wonder if they were born with it and had to become butches — because what else can you do with an attitude like that? — or if they came by it as they grew up — because how else could you survive as a butch lesbian? It's the attitude they need to walk around on the earth and not have boys kill them. It's the attitude they need to survive school. It's lighter stuff, too, like butches can drive you crazy because they don't want you to go on and on and on.

Roxxie: You mean butches don't talk as much?

JoAnn: They don't want to talk about stuff they think is trivial like shoes and earrings. Because butches aren't girls, they don't want to talk about stuff I want to talk about.

We've really messed it up by saying there are only two genders. Femme lesbians really don't fall into the same category as heterosexual women, and butch lesbians aren't boys and aren't girls, so we're not talking about traditional sex roles here either. It's something different.

It's really a mistake to link butches with heterosexual males. It's my experience that butches are interested in pleasing femmes. I don't think men are a bit interested in pleasing heterosexual women. Butches want to make sure things are OK for femmes. Straight men are more into controlling women.

My adage is that the butch is in charge, but I'm the boss. Both butches and femmes like it that way — butches take charge of certain things, but it's the femmes who run the show. That's totally different from how most heterosexuals have their scenes arranged. With butch/femme, there's an important division of top power. My girlfriend's the one who should make sure we're sitting in a good place in a restaurant, but if she doesn't do it, I'm going to move us.

Roxxie: How have things changed since you came out?

JoAnn: Women in their forties and above think that the twenty-somethings have more fluidity than we ever did. But that's because we came out of such a rigid lesbian culture. There's tremendous rigidity and negativity about butch/femme among the forty-year-olds — it's like you're doing something very radical. There's so many rules in my age group.

But I don't believe in the fluidity either. I don't think it's about roles, I think it just IS. It's like some women are lesbians and no matter what they did they'd still be lesbians.

I was always femme and I was always a femme lesbian. I'm so thankful I've lived long enough in lesbian culture to be able to get back to that place inside me where I always was, because in the '70s you could not be a femme at all.

Roxxie: I was talking to someone about how I've somehow circled back to the person I was before I came out, only now I've come back as a lesbian.

JoAnn: I feel that way. My visions have changed, but the way I dress, the way I feel, what I do with makeup and jewelry is much the same as before I came out. Even who I'm attracted to — except I didn't recognize butch lesbians for who they were before I came out.

Roxxie: What kind of self-image do you think butches have?

JoAnn: It's really hard. You don't know how to dress, you don't know how to do your hair, you're not a boy and you're not a girl. You're with boys until what, sixth grade? Then suddenly you're kicked out because you're not a boy, and your parents say, "You're not a boy!" and what do you do? You can't go with the girls because you're not a girl. One thing I've found that's very consistent is that butches became social isolates. They are readers or television addicts. They're loners.

Roxxie: You can play sports.

JoAnn: Sports are great because they build butch self-esteem, and also give femmes a place to go and watch butches play! But there is a whole social thing that butches don't know how to do. For instance, do you go on vacation to South America? Do you go to places where you're supposed to be a girly-girl? Since I'm a femme, I pass in those places. I don't pass when I'm with my girlfriend, but then I don't care.

Roxxie: Do you think butches are more constrained?

JoAnn: I think that's why they're quieter. Femmes get hassled by men, but by the time we've grown up, we know how to get rid of them. But butch lesbians are competition for straight men.

Roxxie: Can straight men learn anything from butches?

JoAnn: Sure. Straight men could learn a lot about how to take care of women both sexually and emotionally.

Roxxie: Is it easier to be a butch woman today than fifteen years ago?

JoAnn: That's an interesting question. I don't think it's any easier, because butch women are still in competition with straight men. That's why it's the responsibility of femme lesbians to come out. Because we can pass, we need to come out in support of our butch sisters. It's in all of our self-interests to create a positive atmosphere for butch lesbians so they're not in therapy for the rest of our lives.

Coming Up Butch

DEBBIE BENDER AND LINNEA DUE

FEMINISM *and a pair of socks loom large in this conversation about growing up butch in the '50s and '60s. Covering ages seven to twenty-five, two women discuss the different accommodations they made to adapt to a world of rapidly changing social definitions that nevertheless did not, during that period, expand enough to encompass them. Debbie Bender, forty-three, is now a maintenance worker in Oakland, California, and Linnea Due, forty-five, is a novelist and journalist who lives in Berkeley.*

Linnea Due: Sometimes when I talk to people about butch/ femme I feel like I'm speaking a foreign language. They seem to have such a different idea of what roles are, which is that they're a matter of style, rather than how you feel, like you can take them on and off. Let's talk first about when we were kids.

Debbie Bender: I always knew that I was going to fall in love with a woman and get married, and all my fantasies involved my being the boy or the husband. By the time I was eight or nine I knew what "gay" meant. I grew up in New York City, so I had a lot of exposure to gay people. My parents were politically and socially very liberal, so they had sexually oriented books around the house, like Henry Miller. They didn't mind me reading them. But my mother was violently homophobic. I had an aunt who had all these gay male friends from work. My mother hated them, but they seemed normal and natural to me.

In recent years I've wondered... it seems like so many women grew up not knowing who they were, grew up confused, feeling like outsiders but not knowing why. Was it harder to *not* know why you were an outsider or harder to know why?

Linnea: I, too — long before I understood what gay meant — knew that I would marry a woman, and I would be the husband. When I was around six, I discovered that was not the usual course of things. I'd get into arguments with kids when I mentioned my wife. "Girls can't have wives," they said. Well, I was going to, even if no one had ever done it before, but that's when I started thinking I might have trouble being who I was. I'd always known I was different. I knew I was a girl, but there was a separation between me and other girls. I almost felt like a third sex, like I was something different. It didn't bother me at first, but the more socialized I got, the more I started worrying.

Debbie: I didn't mind being a girl, but I just flat-out refused to grow up to be a woman. That meant wearing makeup and high heels and girdles. I *did* go through a period where I decided I was going to grow up to be a man, that that would really be the best solution all around. I must have been around seven. I checked in the mirror every day to see if my breasts were growing, and as long as they weren't, I figured that was fine. And I sneaked in behind my father when he peed to see how he did it. I thought that was the big difference. I figured if you practice anything long enough... He was remarkably patient with me, considering that having a small child sneak in every time you take a leak probably freezes you right up. [*Laughter*]

Linnea: I did that same kind of thing. Right around the time I realized things might get difficult, I figured it would be easier if I grew up to be a man, especially if I could skip the boy stage. At that time they were having all those Wonderbread commercials, where they said you could build muscles twelve ways. So I started eating tons of Wonderbread, and my parents were saying, "What's this sudden craze for Wonderbread?" I thought if I ate enough Wonderbread I'd bulk up and turn into a guy. They said, "You don't have to be strong, you're a girl." That was a big disappointment to me. I *wanted* to be strong. I said to them, "Well, can't you be a strong girl?" The gender part was less important to me than being able to be who I was.

When I was around eleven, things started getting bad. I knew by then that my being different and wanting to marry a woman meant I was a lesbian – I'd figured out the label – and I suspected what that was going to mean over the course of my life.

Debbie: Had you read anything? Like had you read *The Well of Loneliness*?

Linnea: Not that, but I'd been stealing *Beebo Brinker* and all those '50s pulp novels out of our little corner grocery store for ages. I also went over to City Lights bookstore in San Francisco to buy *The Ladder*. So I knew that somewhere on this earth there were other lesbians, though I hadn't seen any that I knew of. And I was scared. I was scared of being identified.

Debbie: By your parents? The public?

Linnea: By everyone. It was a terrible secret I had to hide. I was always very poker-faced and non-emotional so I wouldn't give anything away. I thought everything I said might have hidden meanings that would be obvious to other people, so I was very dampened. My biggest priority was keeping people from seeing me. I thought I was doing a good job until I got thrown out of the Girl Scouts for being too masculine –

Debbie: I got thrown out of the Girl Scouts, too, when someone saw me going into a gay club. I was thirteen. I was actually going in to buy a copy of *The Ladder*, not to drink or pick anybody up. So they got me for the right reason for the wrong reason, if you know what I mean. My defense was weak. What could I say, I was looking for someone? I *was* looking for someone. [*Laughter*]

Linnea: My whole world turned upside down. Here I thought I was hiding successfully. What I didn't understand is that my whole *person* was out there. I *was* masculine in that way they didn't like, but it was so much a part of me I didn't know I had to hide that, too. I believed it was just my thoughts I had to cover up, not the rest of me. So I dropped out of sports, because only dykes played sports, and I started dressing in drag, or what I considered drag. I wore makeup, I wore hose all through junior high and high school.

Debbie: It's important to note in an historical context that all of us *had* to wear skirts and dresses. We had very rigid dress codes. It wasn't until the middle of my college years that my primary dress was able to switch to jeans, and even then I couldn't go to my job wearing that. Did you date boys in high school?

Linnea: Yes, and it's something I feel really bad about. I dated this guy, very sweet, who I really liked and who I avoided being alone with. Let's put it this way: If there was a dark room, we weren't in it. I dated him for two years as a cover, and he still won't speak to me, twenty-eight years later.

Debbie: I never really dated boys. Once or twice I tried going out with a guy, just to do it. I started dating women when I was quite young, like fourteen — going out with women, that is, instead of just going out with the girls, on what were clearly dates.

Linnea: Did you approach it like that? Did she know what it was?

Debbie: Yes. We both did. I dated several different women before I got into a serious relationship. I wasn't sexual with the first few women; I was only about fourteen. We were learning. We were still too young to get into the bars. In those days the drinking age was eighteen. By age sixteen everyone had fake ID, but thirteen and fourteen was pushing it. So we rode the buses, we went to movies. I didn't have any money. I began learning how to dress and act butch. I started smoking. I originally learned how to smoke so I could light someone's cigarette. And I stole a pair of my father's socks. Someone growing up today probably wouldn't realize how significant socks were. I had all these girls' socks, which were very different from boys' socks or men's socks. Even if I were wearing a pair of jeans, I didn't have any socks —

Linnea: *Dark* socks.

Debbie: Right. To go with my jeans. That was my big first step in crossdressing. I was about fifteen. I don't remember if my date even knew I had on my father's socks. *I* knew I had on my father's socks, and it was tremendously exciting. I mean it was sexually arousing as well as being emotionally satisfying, an itch I didn't know I had. It was straight downhill from there. [*Laughter*] After that, I got more and more into crossdressing. I was living with my parents in a very small apartment, me and my sister and my mother and father. They had a one-bedroom, with my parents sleeping in the living room. There weren't any closets.

Linnea: So this couldn't be a hidden activity.

Debbie: Well, it *was* completely hidden, because what I did — this sounds much more sordid than it actually was — I had a locker at the bus station. I kept a little suitcase there. I'd go into the restroom and change —

Linnea: Go into the women's restroom —

Debbie: [*Laughter*] Well, yeah, it had its flaws. But I actually didn't get in trouble with that. I was really furtive. I would change shirts, and then I'd come outside and put on a tie and jacket standing in front of my locker. By the time I got out of high school, I wouldn't go out on a date unless I was really dressed up. A few years later, in college, if I were going out on a heavy date, I would completely crossdress. I would bind my breasts, wear men's wing-tip shoes, a nice suit and sometimes a hat, slick back my hair. I always had trouble with my hair.

Linnea: Yeah, we both have unruly hair —

Debbie: When I was in high school, I had it conked. We'd all go down after school and get our hair straightened. Those were the days when women were ironing their hair.

Linnea: So how'd your parents react to all this?

Debbie: When I was twelve, my mother and I started having these really major fights about nothing. I'm sure all adolescent girls have fights with their mothers, but these were really massive, emotionally abusive fights. They didn't make any sense to me at the time. In retrospect, I'm sure it was perfectly clear to her that I was gone. I wasn't going to turn into a little princess. My father didn't want to challenge my mother, so he hung back. By the time I was fifteen, I was spending more and more time away from my parents' house. I would come in at midnight and leave at six to go to school, and on weekends I'd stay at a friend's. My parents were torn. They knew I wasn't shacking up with some boy, and they knew I wasn't about to get pregnant —

Linnea: Weren't taking drugs —

Debbie: Well, I *was* taking drugs, just like everybody else at the time.

Linnea: True, how could I forget? [*Laughter*] You weren't shooting smack.

Debbie: Right. And I think my father must have spent some time pointing out to my mother that she should be counting her blessings. My cousin *was* shooting smack, and she had a baby at fifteen. I was a good student at a good school and I had an afternoon job and I was going to college and I was doing everything I was supposed to be doing —

Linnea: In fact, you were absolutely angelic —

Debbie: Except for this one little problem. [*Laughter*] My mother never really did come to terms with it. And I basically said — and I'm not sure I would do it the same way again because I think it's unnecessarily arrogant — I said, "If you love me, love my lover." After not having contact with them for a number of years, and them still living in this one-bedroom apartment, still sleeping on a couch in the living room — I think this was in 1976 — what I did was quite rude: I brought my lover, her four-year-old son, and the dog to stay in the apartment.

Linnea: My mother was the belle of the ball in her youth, very beautiful, an incredible dancer, with a million boyfriends. I was as unlike that as I could have been. I'm sure I was a tremendous disappointment to her. She didn't see how she could live through who I was — I was like a foreigner. Plus I was much closer to my father. We did all this sports stuff together. We went to games and talked sports all the time. When I was a kid, before I stopped playing softball, I used to practice pitching to him almost every evening.

Debbie: Was it depressing? Did you go through wanting to kill yourself?

Linnea: At age sixteen, I took my '50s pulp novels and burned them in the incinerator. There must have been thirty of them. I had this mad hope that if I didn't think about these things I could somehow change, be someone I wasn't. That resolve lasted less than a week, and it still kills me that I burned those books.

Debbie: I always wanted to be someone else, but I never felt I could. I really have always wanted to be one of the crowd. Given a choice, even today, if there were some switch I could flip and suddenly find myself driving a station wagon full of kids in a carpool out in the suburbs somewhere, I would do it. But it just never has seemed even remotely possible. I couldn't change. It'd be like building your life around winning the lottery.

Linnea: I *was* depressed during my adolescent years, but mostly I drank. I drank phenomenally. Every single night I got drunk enough to pass out, and probably three nights out of seven I was blacked out. My drinking had a lot to do with my hiding. Once I was able to start dressing the way I wanted to and being who I was, my drinking diminished, and I stopped at age twenty-six.

Debbie: That was around Stonewall.

Linnea: No, later. Stonewall was '69, the year I turned twenty-one.

Debbie: But the climate was changing. You and I know that Stonewall was not like throwing a switch. To hear people speak of it in terms of pre-Stonewall or after-Stonewall...

Linnea: There *were* some things that changed quickly though. I got thrown out of college for being gay in January '69, six months before Stonewall. By January '71, women were strolling around campus holding hands.

Debbie: In February or March of '69, I was having an affair with my floor monitor. She got room and board for doing that job, and she needed it. She was thrown out of the dorm for our affair. One of the other students squealed on us, which is what happened to you, too.

Linnea: Even a rumor was sufficient to destroy lives. In our junior high and high school it was like a reign of terror in terms of homophobia.

Debbie: Ours, too. The result for me — in a couple days I'm going back to Chicago for a reunion of people I lived with in college. I lived in that apartment for two years, in '71 and '72, with probably eleven other people. I would bet that half those people don't even know I'm gay. It was not something you would talk about. I would never say, "Well, I'm spending the night with my girlfriend." When I was going out on a date, I would sneak out of the house and do most of my prep work in the car. I'd put on my tie, change shoes, slick back my hair in the car.

Linnea: Did you have butches as role models when you were growing up? I guess the way I learned about how you were supposed to act was from those books. The first time I went to a bar was in December 1968 — I was drunk off my ass, driving down East 14th Street in Oakland — I stopped at a gas station and slicked back my hair. I went blundering in and asked someone to dance, and she just said thanks at the end of the song and walked off. I was crushed. Didn't she want to go home with me? Wasn't that how you did it? I asked this other woman to dance and she *did* want to go home with me. So it worked. [*Laughter*]

Debbie: I guess that's why we did it. It worked.

Linnea: We go to her hotel room — she was living in this crappy hotel in downtown Oakland — and I start making love to her. Making love to a woman was what I'd been fantasizing about for ages. I can't express how excited I was. In the elevator I was all over

her. So I start making love to her, and suddenly she says, "God-damnit! Why do I always pick up butches?" I didn't know what I had done – I didn't know what I was doing to make her say that. Of course, what I was doing was making love to her. I was being really aggressive.

Debbie: Was she butch?

Linnea: I don't know. I guess she was. It turned out fine, I mean, she didn't put up any objections after that. [*Laughter*] But it just shows how naïve I was.

Debbie: Well, I learned partly from role models, from people I'd talk to in bars. The older butches were so protective. They wanted to help. They'd come over and tell you had your cuff links on back-wards, things that were hard to learn.

Linnea: Yeah, you don't have your father showing you. "Dad, how am I supposed to do this?"

Debbie: Exactly. And we had long discussions of various techni-calities. I didn't know any women in those days who routinely wore dildoes for dressing up. But the really stone butches – the ones who wouldn't be touched themselves when they were making love to a woman — would wear Kotex, cut them up, and pad them around. I doubt they owned dildoes or knew what to do with one. But a fair number wore Kotex and we'd have discussions of what kind to use, and how and where to cut it and how to keep it from shifting around.

Linnea: Or socks.

Debbie: Yeah. Socks weren't as popular as Kotex. I don't think Kotex shifted as much, and also I think it pressed better on you, even though they wouldn't admit to wanting stimulation themselves. They'd show you how to bind your breasts and tell you places to buy underwear without being harassed by the sales clerks. So the older butches in the bars were very helpful, but there was also a lot of experimentation. I'd try stuff out, different clothing, with my lover. In those days there was this thing about the three articles of clothing —

Linnea: Sure, the three pieces of clothing of your own sex.

Debbie: Yeah, and everybody claims that it was a law, but nobody can tell you in what state or when it went on the books or off the books. We'd have extended discussions about what would or would not constitute an article of clothing. As if you were gonna sit there and have a half-hour discussion with the cop —

Linnea: While he's beating you up —

Debbie: Yeah, don't beat me! I've got on three articles of clothing! [*Laughter*] I've actually heard it both ways. One was that if you were wearing more than three articles of the opposite sex it was illegal, and the other was that if you weren't wearing three articles of your own sex it was illegal.

Linnea: Maybe because I was older than you were by the time I came to the bars, when people would talk to me, I was defensive. Also this was during the war. I was kind of a hippie, though I wouldn't have called myself that at the time. I was dressed in Navy drag, work shirts and jeans or thirteen-button pants.

Debbie: As much of America was at the time.

Linnea: Yes, but this was not looked upon with favor in the East Oakland bars. People would come up and ask was I against the war or what. I didn't get a lot of help in the bars. But people accepted me as butch even though I didn't know what the hell I was doing. I was sharing a house with this butch named Nance, and she asked me one day if I let my dates make love to me. And I said, "Yeah."

And she said, "Really?" and I said, "Yeah." So she said, "Well, do you think *I* should do that?" And I said, "Yeah, you should, you're missing a big part if you don't."

Debbie: I'm amazed she could even ask.

Linnea: Well, I could have been nicer. I was just very matter-of-fact about it.

Debbie: But that probably was the only thing she could hear. If you'd been nicer about it, it might have upset her more.

Linnea: Could be. Certainly it was clear that I didn't think it was any big deal. So the next day she says, "You were right! That was fantastic!" [*Laughter*] So people *would* talk to me, but I always felt like I was in a weird position where I didn't really fit in.

Debbie: I always felt that way, too. I come from a working-class background, so I could fit in at the bars, but I had to conceal that I'd been to college.

Linnea: So would I. If you mentioned that, it was hopeless.

Debbie: And certainly I had to conceal my feelings about the war. But for me, my big secret, which to some extent is still true, is that even though I am extremely butch and I've been with many femmes and been turned on to them, the women that I'm really attracted to are always somewhat butch. They're usually not as butch as I am, but they're not what I would consider femmes. And that just wasn't done.

Linnea: No, that was bad. I did that, too. People couldn't figure out what was going on with me, and that made them uncomfortable. Another place you had to be in the closet was in the women's movement. I went from closet to closet depending upon which group I was with.

Debbie: Oh, absolutely. It was a nightmare. Over most of my life, I've done work with left organizations. Up until '76 or '77, the gay groups didn't want you because you were political and a woman, the women's groups didn't want you because you were gay and political, and the political groups didn't want you because you were a woman and gay. It didn't matter where you tried to turn your energies, you were in another closet.

But I identified really strongly as a feminist, even while I was growing up. My mother, for all her problems, tried to impress upon me that I could be whatever I wanted. In high school I would get so angry at what girls weren't allowed to do, at the cages we were put into. So when the women's movement started, I said, hot diggity, that's great. And I really feel like over the years the most hurtful and cutting rejections I've had have come from my sisters, primarily in the women's movement and later in the PC lesbian movement. Those are the groups that just cut me dead. In January 1972 my lover and I decided to come out in our women's rap group. We came out individually as we were going around the circle. We said it at the end, and everybody freaked and said, "Oh, we have to go home and think about this." The next week we told them we were sleeping together. After that nobody had to think about anything. "Out, out, both of you," they said. That was my last try at a formal rap group. I decided I would just go for the political and skip the emotional stuff, so I joined my local NOW.

Linnea: The rap group I was in was a lesbian rap group.

Debbie: Well, that made a lot more sense than the way I was doing it.

Linnea: But it didn't. It was equally horrible. There was this group of lesbians — quote unquote lesbians — who were living on Ellsworth Street in Berkeley in a communal house. And these were all political lesbians, like none of them had come out?

Debbie: Oy.

Linnea: I met this woman and got into this CR group. The political lesbians were very up on the right way to be a lesbian. Being butch was really bad.

Debbie: Yeah, we weren't doing it the right way. There was nothing we were doing the right way.

Linnea: When I would open the car door for somebody, I'd get screamed at. When I lit somebody's cigarette, I'd get my face slapped. My lighting someone's cigarette was the most oppressive thing on the earth.

Debbie: Oh, no, more oppressive was if you mentioned that there might be some cute girls at a rally the next day. The worst thing you could do was objectify an entire movement by commenting that you were looking at the women.

Linnea: Whereas my ex and I liked to drive around and look at girls. I didn't think anything of it. But actually, here's where feeling like a third sex comes in. During high school I *was* kind of a chauvinist pig. I thought women were hysterical and illogical. I looked down on women. The only reason *I* was dressing like a woman was for self-protection. Then I had one of those feminist flashes when I was twenty-one. That big thunderclap? I don't remember now what brought it on, but suddenly I thought, women are oppressed, and almost every single part of life revolves around this oppression.

Debbie: That's such a common experience. It's this total reversal of your assumptions. Your whole bedrock collapses.

Linnea: Exactly. Suddenly I was a feminist, committed mind and soul, so it was particularly painful for me to be trashed by people who were also calling themselves feminists. My whole idea of feminism —

Debbie: Was sisterhood.

Linnea: No, was that feminism would allow women to be who they had the potential to be. And that seemed to be almost entirely the opposite of how these people were interpreting it.

Debbie: They thought you had to be a certain way.

Linnea: They thought you had to be who they wanted you to be. I ran a short-story writing group. One woman had passed her story around to some of her roommates, and they'd felt that two of the characters were exhibiting male-identified characteristics — in other words, they were too butch. The woman went through this soul-searching in our writer's group, about how she realized her thinking was polluted because she was too identified with the patri- archy. Other women were making her change her story, a story she was writing from her own experience. They were essentially saying to her that her experience of life was invalid.

Debbie: It hasn't changed.

Linnea: No, it hasn't. So where we thought we would truly find a home was just another closet, and in fact, maybe the worst of all.

Debbie: It *was* the worst because we thought finally there was hope. At that point I decided politics was where it was at. So I ran off to find NOW chapters.

Linnea: But they didn't like you because you were gay.

Debbie: Well, I foolishly admitted I was gay. The NOW chapters would have been perfectly happy if everyone had shut up. My off-the- cuff estimate is that sixty-five percent of every NOW chapter was prob- ably diesel dykes. And they were the most active and doing the best organizing. NOW had some inkling of that and didn't want to hear it.

Linnea: Well, they were being dyke-baited every other second.

Debbie: They *were* being dyke-baited. And the way to answer it would have been to say, "Yes, and they're women, too, so what of

---

it?" instead of quivering and cowering. So I got thrown out of my NOW chapter. I decided a plague on all their houses, and I packed my bags and moved as far out into the countryside on a hippie commune as I could get. I said, "Fuck you all. You don't want me, I don't want you either. I'm going to sit out in the country and vegetate." That lasted about three or four years.

Linnea: That's a significant period of time.

Debbie: So I missed the middle '70s, because I was happy as a clam milking my cows and hoeing my weeds. When I moved back to Boston in the winter of '75, I immediately found that the situation was, if anything, worse. The women's movement was no longer the central focus for me that it had been, but the burgeoning lesbian movement was horrible. You had to dress exactly right, more rigid than the dress codes in high school, talk exactly right, act exactly right, and fuck exactly right.

Linnea: You had to be total little clones.

Debbie: You had to eat the right foods and drink the right drinks. And here I came stomping off the farm, still basically a diesel dyke, still wearing my boots and my black leather jacket, still leaping to light someone's cigarette. I caught enough of the '70s that I was tempted to go back on my farm, back in my shell.

Linnea: What'd you dress in when you came into Boston? It was certainly no longer acceptable to dress high butch.

Debbie: That's true. But my crossdressing more or less reflects the social milieu. Boys going out on dates don't wear a suit or tie anymore either. I used to be able to pass, at least to the extent of walking down the street, taking public transit, in a restaurant, without being hassled. I'd use the men's room. I think now if I dressed in a suit and a tie and tried to take someone out to a restaurant, I'd stand out like a sore thumb. No one dresses like that anymore. So now I might wear a tie, but I'd wear a sports jacket rather than a suit. I still like to dress up, but I guess it looks different.

Linnea: As you get older it's harder to pass. I could pass when I was younger, because I was skinnier for one.

Debbie: Hips —

Linnea: Hips are a problem. But also we look older. When you're in your early twenties, it's not strange that your face is smooth. You just look like a young man. Whereas if you have some gray in your hair, it just doesn't look the same.

Debbie: It's been a real emotional problem for me over the years that most of the world doesn't see me as a woman. If I'm just dressed normal, in jeans and a shirt, probably ninety percent of the world sees me as a guy, addresses me as "Sir," tries to stop me when I use the women's room, hands me the check in the restaurant. It used to be ninety-nine percent, but you're right, now that I'm getting older, it's down to ninety. I cannot explain why I work so hard to make people see me as a man and then it upsets me when they do. It doesn't upset me when I'm dressing for it, it upsets me when I'm just being me.

Linnea: I got off on passing. I would go to the straight bar around the corner and play pool.

Debbie: It was fun cuz you could *do* that. It's kinda wonderful to be able to do those things.

Linnea: I had a moustache, I got dressed up in nice clothes.

Debbie: Did you have trouble with a moustache? I've always had a terrible time.

Linnea: No. I got good stuff from a theatrical supply house. I'd fashion sideburns and the moustache and trim them so they looked sharp. It amazed me that I could walk into that bar two days later in my regular clothes and nobody would ever know.

Debbie: Did you ever pick up a woman while you were passing?

Linnea: No. I was always afraid to do that. I was afraid that she would totally flip out. Women would clearly have been available to be picked up while I was passing, but I wouldn't do it.

Debbie: Cuz they were straight.

Linnea: I'd had some bad experiences, particularly while I was working at the racetrack. One time this woman and I went back to her room, and I started making love to her, and she just completely freaked.

Debbie: She hadn't expected that?

Linnea: No. She knew that's what was going on — it was the point of going to her room. But when push came to shove, she couldn't handle being with a woman. It was pretty awful. And with passing, you'd be misleading someone on top of it. In *Stone Butch Blues*, there's that scene where she's making love to the woman who thinks she's a man. I just can't imagine doing that. I wouldn't like it at all.

Debbie: I have to agree. I've never tried to pick up a woman who didn't know I was a woman. If I was in drag, and I was in a women's bar, then obviously they knew I was a woman.

Linnea: I almost always, in fact, I always passed in straight circumstances.

Debbie: It's easier.

Linnea: Yes, but mostly I would never go in full drag to lesbian bars because so quickly it was completely *verboten*. I remember one of my friends going to a bar in New York on New Year's Eve in '75 and no one would speak to her all night because she was wearing a tux.

Debbie: You'd get in far more trouble. I mean, even if you were discovered in a straight bar, you'd never get in as much trouble as you would in most lesbian bars.

Linnea: I remember going to this heavy role bar called Leonarda's and this group of lesbian feminists organizing a circle dance, running roughshod over whatever social conventions existed at Leonarda's, asking butches to dance or asking femmes to dance without asking the butch —

Debbie: Which isn't all bad.

Linnea: No, but there was no effort to understand what they were doing or who they were dealing with. It was like, "We have the answers here. Let's stop this patriarchal stuff."

Debbie: And do things my way.

Linnea: Exactly. But to me, a lot of that was because they didn't look at lesbianism as sexual. Dancing in a circle is not sexual. Putting across lesbianism as a political statement meant that when you *did* come to sexuality — and lesbianism, after all, *is* sexual — it had to be all soft and sweet and sensitive, and above all, completely equal on every level. So not only could there be no butch/femme or S/M, there could be no difference, period. You couldn't even *dress* differently, even if your dress had no gender identification. This idea that we all dressed butch in the '70s is really rewriting history.

Debbie: You even had to drive a certain type of car. How many lesbians do you know who drive Cadillacs?

Linnea: That sweet sexual expression funneled into the political picture people were trying to create. A lot of it was to make lesbianism palatable.

Debbie: To people who weren't sexually lesbians.

Linnea: Or to straights. And it was also saying, "We have the moral high ground here. We're sensitive and completely equal unlike all the rest of you. We're the only people on the earth who aren't oppressive."

Debbie: I think it also comes from being very young and caught in a cultural matrix that denies history and denies cause and effect. Most of those women truly believed they had invented lesbianism — and in fact, that kind of lesbianism they sort of *had.* They were uninterested in hearing that it's always been around.

Linnea: Because they didn't like the form it's always been around in.

Debbie: Right. It didn't meet their standards. But there really is a cultural thing here, even about passing. If ninety percent of the world thinks I'm a guy, that's the white world. For some reason black people seem to recognize me as a woman. Maybe because there's a higher cultural expectation of strong women. And in other cultures there's a different concept. Some of the heaviest butch/femme I've ever seen is in Filipina bars. And it's also a class thing. It was really clear to me when I moved here that the bars I'd gone to in New York were underground working-class. Some of the bars you're describing are filled with more middle-class, college-educated white women, who are the ones who invented that kind of lesbianism. There are still some of those working-class bars with women acting out butch/femme, still with teased hair.

Linnea: A lot of the hippie movement was middle-class kids in rebellion. But there was also a heyday of bars in East Oakland in the '70s, all role bars — the Jubilee, the Manhole, the Sidetrack, the Chalet. There were after-hours clubs, too, with their two or three fights a night. The gay guys were out fucking in the backyard, and the lesbians were inside knocking the handles off coffee cups so they could gouge each other when the fight started. The guys'd move against the wall and say, "Christ, the dykes are fighting again."

Debbie: I remember bars like that. Rather pleasant, in a way.

Linnea: I was always so drunk at that point that I could hardly keep track of what was going on. So there you were in Boston.

Debbie: Yes, and remember how I said I wanted to be one of the crowd? Well, shortly after I arrived in Boston, I met the woman with the kid and the dog. Only a couple weeks after I began dating her, she was in a terrible car accident. She was going to be laid up for months, and they were planning to send her kid to a foster home. I had to do something, so I moved in and started supporting her.

Linnea: That must have been so strange. You'd just been dating.

Debbie: It ended up OK. We managed to stay really good

friends. It was the ultimate butch/femme fantasy. I was working two jobs with a wife and a kid and a dog. I always said I wanted to be part of the herd, but sometimes I felt like screaming, "This wasn't what I meant!"

Linnea: Of course, men probably feel the same way.

Debbie: I often wondered if straight men have that trapped feeling, if one day they wake up and find themselves with a wife and two or three kids and everyone's working and struggling. It made me more sympathetic to them.

Linnea: After I came out in December '68, I suddenly decided I had to change my major. I couldn't be a writer; I had to go into pre-law or pre-med because I was going to have to support someone. I was ecstatic and devastated at the same time, as if I'd finally accepted who I was only to lose myself in another way. Luckily only a couple days later I started sleeping with the woman who is still my closest friend, and I thought, "I don't have to support her. She's perfectly capable of supporting herself." I was so thrilled I didn't need to become my father.

You were working at the shipyard then, right? How did the people there treat you?

Debbie: The people at the shipyard never got over the fact that I was a woman to get around to the fact of what kind of woman I was.

Linnea: I know exactly what you mean. Some of the guys at the racetrack would do everything they could to try to convince me I couldn't do the job.

Debbie: Physically, it was exhausting. The older guys were OK, and the younger ones who were my age, who'd just gotten out of 'Nam, were totally fucked–up and doing all kinds of drugs and having flashbacks. Women at the yard didn't matter to them. It was the men who weren't recent veterans and who were young that were the problem.

But I was in this car pool with one black guy and two older white guys. This was during busing, and Boston was going up in flames. People were throwing firebombs at buses with little babies on them. I'd go put our boy on one of those buses every morning, and then I'd ride in this car pool, thinking about him on the bus. We'd drive through the streets of Boston, me and the black guy and the white guys. A lot of life is like that. How'd I miss how strange that was?

Conversation with
a Gentleman Butch

An Interview with Jeanne Cordova

LILY BURANA

THE *following interview with Jeanne Cordova was conducted in her lovely Hollywood home. Present during our chat was Jeanne's lover Lynne, the perfect smart-femme complement to Jeanne's sharp, gentlemanly butchness. We gabbed amiably about history, herstory and butchness through the decades.*

Jeanne Cordova: Among heavy-duty butches, there's always been butch/butch coupling. My first lover was butch. She was from Pico Rivera, which is a Mexican ghetto, and she had these little pointy-toed shoes, and I just thought she was adorable! When I was younger, there was no one more baby-butch than myself, so I had crushes on older butch women. I would've slept with any of them if they'd asked me! I thought, well, it's probably just role-modeling, but where's the fine line drawn between role-modeling and sexual attraction?

I've often struggled with myself over my attraction to other butches. If I like femme women so much, how can I still be attracted to butch women? I now acknowledge my desires as such: I major in femmes and minor in baby butches.

I think every butch should definitely sleep with other butches, at least in the coming-out period. My friend Robin Tyler, who was kind of my mentor as a butch, had what she calls the "academy for young butches."

She'd pick up a young butch at some political meeting or something, take her home so she could top her in bed. She'd show her how to dress right, and she'd show her the manners, how to use dildoes, etc. She did this for me when I was twenty-one, so I learned all this shit from her, and then I "graduated."

Lily Burana: So this was kind of like a finishing school for butches? Like in the gay men's S/M community, when an older top man would take on a novice and turn him out?

Jeanne: Yes, but the men would make a whole relationship out of that. You don't find that kind of institutionalization of mentoring among butch women.

Lily: In Los Angeles, there always seems to be a shortage of butches.

Jeanne: Well, see, we don't find that a problem! [*Laughter*] Among butches of the same age group there might be a sense of competition. Certainly Robin Tyler, Jean O'Leary — another friend of mine — and I, when we lived together, had to make a rule that whoever saw a girl first had first rights, because we were often competing for the same woman. But it was still thorny; we'd fight over women.

One of my tips for butches is that if you want to have other butches as friends, you have to lay down some ground rules. If you're going to compete with each other, it's going to ruin your friendship.

Lily: What other advice would you have for nascent butchlings?

Jeanne: Well, like I said, I think they should go to bed with each other for a spell. Number one: It teaches you something about power in bed, because most femmes don't exercise their power in bed like butches do. And it also teaches you a sense of your own limits. A lot of butches, let's face it, are bottoms, and I think butches who *are* ought to make the most of it, because there's a lot of top femmes who want that.

The hardest thing that I've had to deal with being butch, short of out-and-out battering on the streets, is recognizing who I am as a man and a woman. When I was very young, I didn't have a clue as to who I was gender-wise. I said, "I must be a guy trapped in a woman's body." Then along came feminism, and I said, "No, I'm just a woman, a different kind of woman, that butch kind of woman." More recently, in the last ten years, I've decided that I'm both a man *and* a woman, that I have strong elements of both genders.

A lot of butches will pretend to be men ... but I've found that a lot of femmes like butches *because* we're women. They may like all the leather shit, and jumping on the back of a bike, and being thrown around in bed, but they essentially want to be with women.

When I first got wind that my femme lovers really liked my female body, it was kind of hard for me. I remember distinctly being shocked that my femme lovers loved my breasts. That really gave me pause for thought. It was actually very healing for me. I thought, if *they* like me, maybe *I* should like me. I had to realign my acceptance of my body as a woman's. I think every butch denies her body, and that is a little schizophrenic.

Lily: Do you feel some of the pressures that men do around not being particularly emotive or vulnerable?

Jeanne: I think that when a young butch woman comes of age, she looks around to men for her role models and over-identifies with male crap. I think a lot of us butches model our personalities after some of the worst characteristics of men, and then as we mature, we leave that behind and reclaim some of the female characteristics we denied before.

Since it's often difficult for butches growing up, what with the stigma, it can make butches wall off in the way they deal with society. When they wall off with their lovers, I think some of that is genetic. And I think that's one reason why butches have to struggle more than most femmes to pick up some of those softer virtues that make for healthy living and better relationships.

Lily: What about the sexual stone butch? Do you think she views sexual pleasure as being too vulnerable, or has she internalized a misogyny that would equate admission of sexual pleasure with degradation?

Jeanne: To me, penetration does not equal vulnerability, because I like vulnerability, and I don't like penetration. Some people might call me a stone butch, even though I get off regularly and insist upon it. But I'm also an easy lay, so I can get off practically walking down the street. If the butch psyche doesn't want to identify the body as female, then penetration seems an unnatural act. See, penetration goes with that whole "I'm being taken" idea, and that's not where butch sexuality is.

Now I feel real different about ass-fucking. To me, that's penetration, but I hold it differently than vaginal penetration. I think a lot more butches would be into ass-fucking, but ass-fucking seems

to be anathema in the lesbian subculture. We haven't gotten into our asses as women yet.

Emotional vulnerability is real important. I think that a younger stone butch, emotionally stone, who doesn't want anything to do with her feminine side, is really male-identified. I don't think that's a fully realized butch. That's just aping one form of man, and because I don't think much of men, especially emotionally, I think it's less of a life. So I encourage butches to go out and develop some kind of femme inside themselves and then put it into their butch identity, because then they'll like themselves, and the women they go with will like them better.

I made up this ideal femme, this sort of twin self, and I've gotten to know her a little bit. I have conversations with her; her name is Jennie, and I got to know how she would act, what she would do in a situation.

You're not going to get a quality woman and keep her unless you can access your emotional vulnerability. I also think I was with a lot of power femmes who would drag it out of me.

Lily: It's been said that butch women are a gender all their own, like effeminate men. How does one maintain one's sanity being part of a gender minority in a culture that only recognizes two genders?

Jeanne: The simplest way is to spend a lot of time with your own, in your own. It really does help to build your own culture and your own society. Whenever I need support, I form a group, so I formed a butch mafia. It was just a bunch of us, and we just hung out a lot together, as a sort of sophisticated political gang, and we would have sex talks.

Being with a femme who understands what a butch is can go a long way. I've been with all kinds of femmes, and most kinds of butches, too, and I learned that there's only one kind of lesbian femme who gets that a butch is male *and* female. And you can call it another gender because it amounts to that. When I've been with women who treated me like a man, both in and out of bed — you know, at first I thought, "Isn't this wonderful?" — but it didn't quite fit. I had this girlfriend whom I could tell put me in the same gender category as a straight man. She saw me as totally other than herself. It's alienating. There are some lesbian femmes who really do get it, who really are what I call the true lesbian femmes. If you're butch, I think it's necessary to pick a woman who on some level can validate your masculinity, and feel comfortable with it, and like it.

Lily: What's it like in the het world? Do you think it's loosened up at all?

Jeanne: I don't know that it's gotten that much easier for an easily identifiable butch. We were sitting in a restaurant just the other day, and this has happened to me so many times I don't usually even think about it…. They'll look at me and I'll hear, "What is it?" Then they'll look at Lynne. They'll see a normal-looking straight woman. Then they'll look back at me, and they'll say, "Oh, a lesbian. Dyke." Then they'll look at her and say, "What is she doing with *her*?" Now I just look at them as if to say, "You're right!" and then I might put my hand on her thigh, just to rub it in. I'd like to say it's better that it used to be, but I don't know that it is, all that much.

Butches, to the straight world, are the real lesbians, and femmes, like butch gay men, are not really gay, they're just in a phase, and only the queens are really gay.

Lily: So there's a similarity between butches and queens.

Jeanne: There is, and it's a shame that we don't have more in common, but visually, it represents the genderfuck. I'm the revolutionary who says, "I'm the one who has stepped outside what you've told me to be and thrown it in your face."

Until butches and queens are safe on the streets, the movement really hasn't done what its core is all about. When I was in activism, I would be passed over to go on television because I was butch, and our movement participates in this butch-phobia. It's sort of a strange homophobia. It always comes back to fuck us in the end.

Lily: Why is that?

Jeanne: Because that's not who we are! This whole assimilation-ist thing that says, "We're really just like you except for what we do in bed" – that's garbage. The opposite is true, I think. It's only in bed that we do the same things as straights. The rest of what we do is totally different – how we think, how we feel, how we walk, how we relate to each other, our culture. Until butches and queens are accepted, then society has not changed about gender roles. When they look at you, and it's so important for them to decide if you're male or female that they can't even enjoy their pancakes...

Lily: Well then, it's not about how you have sex, it's about gender.

Jeanne: I think so.

Lily: Why not the sex? Why the gender?

Jeanne: It's so firm to straights. It's like the sun rising in the east and going down in the west. It's an archetype that we threaten. When we go on TV, we should put on the meanest-looking butches and the nelliest men. Then we'd get some progress, which brings me to why I think this new queer movement is so critical. I know a lot of people don't understand that the queer politic goes beyond femi-nism and cuts to the chase. While I still think it's important to say that a lesbian identity is very different from a gay male identity, I think the queer movement is the most important thing that's hap-pened since AIDS or since feminism.

ROSA BONHEUR

ROSA, THE GREATEST ANIMAL PAINTER OF THE 19th CENTURY, HAD SPECIAL RELATIONSHIPS WITH TWO WOMEN: **NATALIE MICAS**, WHO LIVED WITH ROSA UNTIL HER DEATH IN 1889. THEY HAD A GERTRUDE-AND-ALICE TYPE RELATIONSHIP; ROSA PAINTED, AND NATALIE DID THE COOKING. **ANNA ELIZABETH KLUMPKE**, A YOUNG AMERICAN PAINTER FROM SAN FRANCISCO, MOVED IN WITH ROSA,

DURING THE LAST YEARS OF HER LIFE. IN A LETTER TO A FRIEND, ROSA REFERS TO HER AS "MY WIFE."

ROSA AND GEORGE HAD TO GET SPECIAL DISPEN-SATIONS FROM THE GOV-ERNMENT TO WEAR MEN'S CLOTHING. THIS TRANSLATES: "PERMISSION FOR TRANSVES-TITISM."

(The three lovers are buried in one crypt in Père LaChaise cemetery in Paris.)

ROSA'S IDOL AND ROLE MODEL WAS **GEORGE SAND**, 20 YEARS HER SENIOR. (See "FAMOUS FRENCH CROSS-DRESSING BELLES OF THE EPOQUE," #2 OF THE SERIES.) AFTER THE SECOND FRENCH REVOLUTION, BOTH WO-MEN DECLARED THEM-SELVES COMMUNISTS.

WHEN POSING FOR HER PORTRAIT OR DRESSED TO RECEIVE THE MEDAL OF HONOR FROM EMPRESS EUGENIE, ROSA FORSOOK HER UNIFORM OF SMOCK, TROUSERS AND BOOTS FOR THE 19th CENTURY EQUIVALENT OF GERTRUDE STEIN'S SUIT.

GORGEOUS LETTERS BY ANGELA BOCAGE ... Trina Robbins '93

120

Butchiest Dyke Contest

Achy Obejas

The Butchiest Dyke Contest was held at Paris Dance in Chicago, May 1993.

"**MISTY?** A butch named Misty?" Vernita Gray said in utter dismay. She leaned over the railing around the dance floor and stared incredulously at the seven women lined up to compete in this year's Butchiest Dyke Contest.

Some of the women were smoking cigarettes and posing in their softball jackets and tee-shirts. One woman carried a riding crop. Another kept wiping her nose on her arm and grabbing her crotch.

"How the heck can you have a butch named Misty?" asked Gray, last year's winner of Paris Dance's contest.

"Yeah," said Roberta Gray, no relation to Vernita, as she sipped from a sweaty long-neck. "Butches should be named Rusty or Stevie or Champ or something like that. Not Misty — man, that's femmey."

Out under the hot lights, Misty, long hair tied back, decked in leathers and flannel, was gamely getting ready to do the Walk. The Walk — a nonverbal part of the program — was designed to show coolness. A trio of judges — one femme and two androgynous types (lovers, actually) — kept score.

"Last year people were dropping their pants to show off their boxer shorts," said Vernita Gray. "Shit, I didn't do that. I just wait for the women to come to me." She winked. "That's the essence of it, you know — the kind of confidence, a sense of your true woman's self."

ACHY OBEJAS

The first butch — a cigarette-smoking softball player from a team called (Your Worst) Nightmares — strutted and jived across the floor with a winking, sure sense of calm. The next contestant, a handsome Latina in a blue blazer, shyly stepped through the line and shuffled across.

"Man, that woman's confused," said a young woman in a leather jacket hanging over the rail. "She's not a butch. She's just wearing a blazer."

Karen Hutt, a tall, sweet-faced woman in a sweater and dress pants, at thirty-five one of the oldest contestants, was next. She walked straight over to the judges and asked them individually if they cared to dance.

"That's her — that's my successor," said Gray, smiling. "She might not make it with this crowd," — Hutt, like Gray, was black, and most of the audience was white — "but she's the only one up there who gets it."

The next contestant, Jan — a red-haired, freckled Huck Finn type — doffed her shirt in one quick move and, amidst catcalls and whistles, paraded over to the judges in her black bra, flexing her biceps.

"Take it off! Take it off!" someone yelled. "God, if you're going to go that far just go all the way — otherwise what's the point?"

All through the contest, emcee Tracy Barrientos grilled the contestants on the roots of their butchness, their butch behavior, their butch ethics. The younger contestants consistently said they were man-like. The Nightmares contestant said she knew she was butch when she refused to wear dresses in Catholic school and preferred to play with Tonka trucks. Jan declared she liked nothing feminine, "nothing that girls did." Still another contender referred to women as "bitches," drawing boos and hisses from the nearly all-woman audience.

"Man, you can see why I won last time," Gray said disgustedly, and walked off to get a drink.

Only Hutt and Rhonda Craven, the only other African American competitor, went out of their way to affirm their gender. "To me, being butch is being in touch with your masculine as well as your feminine side," said Craven, who wore both a tie and a double-headed axe, a matriarchal lesbian symbol, "but to always be all woman."

"Being butch is not copying men," Hutt said, "but digging deep inside your womanhood to be strong."

Finally it was Misty's turn. Out in the crowd, her three roommates started chanting, "Work it, girl! Sashay! Shante!" As Misty took her first tentative steps, the three burst out laughing.

"She's the most femme person in the entire world," said Cathleen, one of the roommates.

"Yeah, in real life she wears silk undies and dresses," said Michelle, another roomie.

"Everybody in the bar knows her as a femme," said Cindy, the third roommate. "We thought the contest gave her an opportunity to show off a part of her personality that had been closeted for a long time."

"The jacket's mine," said Cathleen, watching Misty inch along straight-faced, "and the suspenders belong to a friend of ours."

"The denim shorts are mine," said Michelle, "and the boots are borrowed."

"But I think the flannel's hers," said Cindy. "Yeah, the flannel's hers. I'm sure of it."

By the time Misty made it back to her starting point the bar was rocking with laughter.

Even Vernita Gray was laughing good-naturedly. "Man, I gotta teach these girls a thing or two," she said, and walked across the floor with a combination sashay and pimp strut that drew thunderous applause.

The contest was the brainchild of Paris owner Linda Rodgers, who said, "I do the contest because I'm sick of the idea that suddenly everybody in the lesbian and gay movement has to look respectable by heterosexual terms. We don't all look 'normal,' whatever that is, and we don't all want to assimilate. And I think butches are a wonderful part of our culture and our history — and they need to be acknowledged."

But as contest time, eight p.m., rolled around, it looked like butches might be extinct. Every woman at Paris was tuned in to the two TVs broadcasting the final episode of "Cheers." Barrientos couldn't get anyone to sign up.

"Well, I wasn't going to do it at all," admitted Craven, "but then I realized there were a couple of younger women who wanted to do it but weren't sure. And I thought, well, if I do it, maybe they'll do it."

More or less the same thing happened to Hutt, who was just in with her lover, Therese Quinn, for a drink and some company. "She's a wonderful butch," Quinn said dreamily. Hutt, standing next to her, beamed.

"You know, I'd like to get a group of butches together and deprogram them from all this male stuff," Hutt said. "All this talk about 'the women' and 'the bitches' — like they're a different species. That's silly. If you're a true butch you know how to be gentle, how to be kind."

At the judges' table, Git, a middle-aged woman who could pass for a TV mom, was busy tallying scores. "I don't like to identify as butch or femme," she said, "but in this case it was about the stereotype."

"It was about a certain toughness," said Xio Lescano, another judge.

Just as the judges were finishing, René Contreras and Elizabeth Zuverink suddenly appeared. Contreras, wearing a skullcap and greasepaint from head to toe, looked like an intergalactic butch elf. Zuverink was dressed only in cutoffs and a pair of roses on a string to cover her nipples.

"The contest started at eight?" said Contreras. "Wow, man, we thought it started at nine."

Vernita Gray looked at her watch, laughing. "It's eleven."

"Wow, like, we thought, you know, we'd enter in the dare-to-wear category, you know?" Contreras continued.

The Nightmares contestant was poking her fingers into the roses on Zuverink's chest and leaning down to smell them. "Very nice," she said. "Oh yes, very nice!"

"This is a butch contest, for Christ's sakes," said a woman in overalls. "What the hell category is 'dare-to-wear'?"

"Gosh, we spent all night getting it together for this," Contreras protested as Zuverink leaned provocatively against the railing, lifting a stiletto heel slightly off the floor.

Finally Barrientos and Gray announced that Hutt, Huck Finn, and the Nightmares woman had been selected as finalists. The winner would be determined by audience applause after each described her favorite fantasy.

"Come on, baby, give us something butch," Gray exhorted the Nightmares woman, who only produced a cliché: an island of Amazons and lots of sex. Gray rolled her eyes.

Hutt directed her fantasy at her lover. It involved Amsterdam, Venice, lesbian gondoliers, moonlight, promises of commitment, and multiple orgasms. The crowd exploded in applause, stomping and whistling. Gray nodded in approval.

That left Huck Finn, who said her fantasy had already come true, and she couldn't reveal the details.

"Give us dirt!" the crowd chanted. "Give us raunch!"

Huck Finn took the microphone and tried to spin out a scene that included parking lots, police sirens, and dinner at Geja's.

"Ah shit — thirty dollars for fried food," muttered Gray.

Hutt won by roaring acclaim. Her prize was fifty dollars and a red coronet strikingly similar to the Imperial Margarine crown.

Quinn looked on proudly. "The others were a little young," she said. "They need to be around older dykes more, butches who can share with them some words of wisdom."

In the corner Misty and her roommates were laughing. Misty had lost the leather jacket and was busy flipping her wrists and giggling.

Huck Finn was sulking. "I'm butchier than her," she said. "I mean, she's wearing earrings. I'm butchier, I'm butchier."

"She just doesn't get it," said Roberta Gray. "At all."

She Strips to Conquer

An Interview with J., Butch Sex Worker

Lily Burana

To the discriminating, butch-appreciative eye, J. is a real dreamboat. Along with her delightful surface appearance — wide, deep-set eyes, heavy brows, angular bone structure, and a glistening set of chompers boasting incisors pointy enough to cut glass — is an engaging personality. J. is easy-going, reflective and funny, character attributes that make her an excellent interview subject. She is not at all defensive about her seemingly contradictory career choice. To pull down cash, J. slips off the butch gear and slides into spikes and lingerie and works femme to the limit in the sex industry.

Lily: Tell me a bit about your background.

J.: I grew up poor in the Bronx. I'm Jewish American; my grandparents were immigrants. The neighborhood I grew up in was predominantly Puerto Rican, and the schools I went to were mixed, but largely Puerto Rican and African American. I left home when I was fourteen. I stayed in school and graduated with the highest SAT scores in my class. School was the one thing I poured my energy into. That and sex, because I really thought that school was my ticket out of my neighborhood, away from my family, poverty, the whole thing.

Lily: When you were a teenager, were you primarily lesbian-identified?

J.: No, not at all. I was totally hetero until I got to California in 1985, the summer that I turned seventeen. Suddenly, I realized I had something to deal with.

Lily: Was it easy to come to grips with being attracted to women?

J.: No. I always knew that I was attracted to women, but I just didn't deal with it. I just kind of put it on a shelf, and when I got to college I started having all these crushes. I lived in this huge student co-operative, and I got crushes on the women who lived there. It was really frustrating because a lot of them would fool around with me, but only once they were really drunk or wasted on their particular drug of choice. In the morning they wouldn't want to remember it, or talk about it, and I wanted something that was more than that, or I at least wanted to be with someone who wasn't so hung up about it that she had to be wasted on Quaaludes to do anything. It was hard because I didn't know where to meet people who were out and comfortable about it, I didn't know where to find it.

Then I moved to Santa Cruz, partly because I liked the school better and partly because I heard there was this huge lesbian community there. Little did I know it was not the kind of lesbian community I would fit into! But it was the only one I knew of, and sure enough, during my first quarter I took introduction to feminism, and in that class I met my first partner with whom I had sex without being drunk.

Lily: So how did you discover that you didn't fit in Santa Cruz?

J.: I was questioning whether I still wanted to sleep with men, or whether I was going to be a dyke, or bisexual, or what. To most of the women there, it was not acceptable to sleep with men. And I started doing sex work. I started doing phone sex first. Most of the women had a problem with even just that. So between those things, it just didn't work.

Lily: Did you start unearthing a more butch identity in Santa Cruz or were you still pretty conventional looking?

J.: I wouldn't say I looked conventional…. I went through this gradual transformation where I looked different every six months. When I left the Bronx I had this huge head of permed hair and makeup on my face. I shaved my hair into a mohawk, and then I had a different color every week, and all kinds of crazy stuff

Lily: Tell me about your first sex work experience.

J.: Phone sex was the first sex work that I ever did — I was nineteen. It was totally a survival matter; I was literally not being able to buy food. And really, I'd been thinking of doing it since I was thirteen years old. I thought, wow, I have this stuff that I can sell, and people will pay me a lot of money for it. What stopped me, really, were the fears pumped into me by this culture about what prostitution was, and thinking I was going to run into some psycho who was going to murder me and leave me in pieces in a hotel room, or whatever.

Lily: How much did you make doing phone sex?

J.: When it was busy, I could make twenty dollars an hour, sometimes maybe even twenty-five. When it was slow, I made nothing, because I got paid per call, so if the phone wasn't ringing, forget it.

Lily: What made you decide to stop doing phone sex and start doing other kinds of sex work?

J.: I did phone sex for four or five years before I did any of the other stuff. Basically, it was just not enough money anymore. I graduated college, and my student loans were due. I was really in debt, and I was hungry. Initially, I thought if I could just be me, as butch as I am, and still be a sex worker, I wouldn't have a problem with it. For a long time I wasn't willing to put on the makeup and the girl clothes and shave my body hair and stuff. It just finally got to the point where I decided that it was more humiliating to be broke all the time than it was to dress in femme drag.

Lily: So what was the first type of performing sex work you did?

J.: Before I danced, I did outcall [prostitution]. I started by answering ads in the personal section of the local weekly paper, and I talked to five guys, and ended up getting together with three of them. I hoped they would all turn out to be long-term clients, but it didn't work out that way. They were all one-timers.

I was so careful about it. I met them for lunch and we talked forever before I agreed to get together with any of them. Once I finally did it, I remember coming home on the bus from the first session and laughing all the way, thinking about how easy it was. How it was nothing like anybody told me it was going to be. I just felt great having that money in my pocket after half an hour's time.

Lily: Did you start placing your own ads after that? How did you promote yourself to convey your butchness?

J.: Well, I started by placing an ad in the local gay paper! When I first started, I wanted to cultivate a different market — either women who were willing to pay for it, or bi guys, or gay guys who were into experimenting, or anyone who would be into me the way I was. My ad said, "k. d. lang isn't for hire, but I am." It did really well! Something about androgyny and blah, blah, blah. But I didn't get that much business from it. A lot of curious people, but not that many following through. I had some clients come through, all men though.

There was one guy who was on the straight side of bi, but he was closeted about it. He really just wanted to be with a woman who would understand him, who was comfortable with the totality of him. We talked for almost half the time we spent together. He was really nice, but I never heard from him again.

I've thought about advertising in *On Our Backs* or other places where I might reach a female market, but I have a feeling there would be more money going into the ad than coming out.

Lily: Why do you think that is? Why aren't women customers of the sex industry?

J.: For a lot of reasons. Women don't have as much money, and women are socialized to be more up-tight in general. And the advertising isn't geared towards them. Most women see something like *Hustler* as being so offensive and foreign that they can't picture themselves being a patron of that kind of industry.

Lily: It would be cool to have a butch escort service.

J.: Totally, but it might not work. You know, women are also socialized to be more relationship-oriented.

Lily: So, you realized there are some financial limitations to perusing an "alternative" sex work angle?

J.: Yes. When I decided that in order to start making some real money I would have to get serious about it, I talked to all my friends who did sex work, then put the ad in the straight weekly. Even then, my ad was a little different than the usual. My ad described me as "boyishly beautiful busty bi woman…" I got a lot of guys who wanted to be with a woman who looked like a lesbian.

Lily: Did you ever turn out in butch drag for these guys?

J.: Fairly often, yeah. I mean, that bi guy I met through the gay paper, when I met him, I showed up in my combat boots. I didn't have on any makeup. I think I still had my flat-top. He was into it, it was cool.

For the other guys, when they say they want someone who looks "like a lesbian," my impression is that they want a lipstick lesbian. They don't really mean hard-core butch. So I still femme it up a little, but not in the extreme.

Lily: What made you decide to go from hooking to dancing?

J.: I haven't stopped doing outcall, it's just not my main source of income.

I did the outcall for a year. I went to New York, and I worked in an old-time brothel, like something you would see in the movies, and that was really interesting. I got back to San Francisco, and I worked some in a house, but I felt kinda burnt on it. Then the woman I worked for got busted. I got really scared because I knew the police had seized all her records — and that included my name and phone number. A client I knew from there called to warn me, so I changed my phone number. I decided that I needed to do something else because I'd had enough obstacles all my life; I didn't need to add something like an arrest to all of them.

Lily: Yeah, the difference between outcall and dancing is that it's unlikely that you'll ever get arrested dancing, as dancing is quasi-legal, but prostitution is totally illegal.

J.: Sometimes it's easier to do outcall, cuz it's one-on-one, and it's done in an hour or less, and you've made your money. Dancing is much more strenuous. You're there for eight hours, the money just sort of trickles in, and there's no guarantee as to how much you'll make on any given day.

Lily: When you started dancing, presumably you didn't have stacks of girlie lingerie, so how did you acquire that?

J.: Well, I already had some for the outcall. I got my first pair of heels down at the thrift store, for five or six bucks. They were almost brand new, and I'm still wearing them. I felt totally hysterical trying them on in the store. I was looking around to see if anyone I knew was there, if anyone was watching me. A femme friend gave me some lingerie, I got donations from people, and bought a few things.

Lily: Do you think it's easier to do sex work in a situation where your clients aren't people that you'd otherwise meet, say, in your personal life?

J.: Yeah, something really weird happened once — I met a client I really, really liked. It flipped me out! I saw him once or twice, and then we both just felt too weird. He just stopped calling, I think because he felt too uncomfortable. I keep hoping we might run into each other somewhere, which we might, because we have a lot of friends in common. In any other circumstance, we might have been friends.

In general, my customers are people who I'd ordinarily have nothing to do with, so it makes the boundaries real easy to keep clear.

Lily: Are you bisexually-identified? Are the partners in your personal life straight-identified, or is it more of a queer thing?

J.: (*Points to her bi-pride tee-shirt, laughing*) I identify as queer, and sometimes I fuck men who happen to be straight, it just happens. It's hard for me to keep the strong limitations around who I will and will not fuck based on how they identify...

Lily: What's the difference between who you might see as a client and who you might see in your personal life?

J.: Well, the straight men that I see in my personal life tend to be musicians with long hair and tattoos, or shaved heads and piercings. The guys I see as clients tend to be paunchy, middle-aged business men, you know, awkward, with glasses.

Lily: Is there stuff you won't do as a sex worker?

J.: I haven't yet spent an entire night with someone. I don't know that I ever would. There are specific sexual things that I save for my friends, like I love getting fisted. I've had a couple clients who wanted to do that to me, and I said no. That's reserved! I also only do anal sex with friends. Partly because with a client it's too risky, and partly because I prefer to keep some things for myself.

Lily: How open are you about being a sex worker?

J.: I'm fairly open — my mother knows! Generally, if there's someone I'm interested in romantically or socially, I let them know pretty soon cuz I feel like they have to be able to deal with it and accept it or I can't be bothered. There are certain situations where I'm quiet about it.

Lily: Do other butch women give you shit about being a sex worker?

J.: I don't know. I think they're more surprised than anything. I've had a lot of butch women tell me I'm not a real butch anyway, so I guess the sex work just follows in that vein.

Lily: Being a sex worker would make you less butch?

J.: Well, yeah. A traditional old-school butch can't understand how I could ever put on heels, or a garter belt...

Lily: ...or even be bisexual.

J.: Right.

Lily: Do you work with other butch women at the theater?

J.: I've only ever seen one, maybe two women who I would consider butch. There was this woman, and I've only seen her there once...she was leaving as I was coming in, and we just kind of looked at each other. There was this sort of acknowledgment. She was slicking her hair back and putting on her jeans... she was butch and she was hot! By and large, they're all pretty femme.

Lily: Do the femme queer women you work with respond to

you as a butch? Have any of them come on to you?

J.: I haven't really had that happen yet. In fact, it's really hard for me to tell who's a dyke or who's bi.

Lily: So you groomed yourself as a femme when you were growing up...

J.: Yes. But I wouldn't say I was femme-identified, I would say I was just clueless.

Lily: Does dressing up femme for work now feel like a return to the old days, like you've come full-circle?

J.: Oh, my god, NO! It's costume now, it's drag. It's theater. I know the femme drag is not really me! I feel a lot more confident about it, too. When I was younger, I was so insecure, wanting to be beautiful and thinking that no matter what I did, there was still something wrong somewhere. Now, I totally have an attitude about it. I have so much more understanding about doing it and what it means, and I can play with that.

Lily: Does doing femme drag for work threaten your butch identity in your personal life?

J.: It did at first. It freaked me out. I'd go out and work at this house for three days, hanging around in femme drag, and then I'd come home and attend some dyke event at a club, and I'd be there surrounded by dykes, feeling really out of balance, very strange.

I'm switching back and forth more easily now. I know that when work is over, the heels come off, the boots go on, and I'm back to being me.

Lily: Do you get calls from women?

J.: I've gotten calls from women who are curious and who just want to talk. I did get a call the other day from a woman who's twenty-two and just coming out. She's not had sex with a woman yet, and she wants to pay me to be her first experience! I'm so psyched!

Lily: Are you going to do it butch-to-femme or femme-to-femme?

J.: I don't know, I'll ask her what she prefers. Isn't that hot?

Lily: If you could work totally as a butch, would you?

J.: Fuck yeah! I think it would be fun to do femme drag occasionally just to confuse people and give them something to think about. But yeah, if I could be a butch stripper, I'd love to. I'd love to have a different female image out there that's hot. But I just don't think I could do it in the world as it stands right now. I couldn't go into the theater and strip in butch clothes. They'd throw me out!

The Joys of Butch

Susie Bright and Shar Rednour

S **USIE** *Bright and Shar Rednour met when Susie was the editor of* On Our Backs. *Her book* Susie Sexpert's Lesbian Sex World (Cleis Press, 1990) *had just been published. Shar, a twenty-seven-year-old writer, had just moved to California and was working at a preschool where she fell in love with Aretha, Susie's daughter. Over diapers and fashion crises, they discovered their mutual respect for, annoyance with, and love of butch women. Since then, Shar has worked as an editor at* On Our Backs, *and has become well known as San Francisco's renaissance femme writer/fashion designer/promoter and general femme spokesperson. Susie, who at thirty-five is known as a lesbian sexpert, has continued to pioneer erotic thought and practice in her book* Susie Bright's Sexual Reality: A Virtual Sex World Reader (Cleis Press, 1992), *and in her articles in* The New York Times, Esquire, *and* Playboy.

Susie Bright: Tell me about your first butch lover.

Shar Rednour: My first butch date and fuck would have been Emily. She was really nice for a first date because she picked me up in a car and was on time and totally appreciative of my femme ways. She wasn't an androdyke who says, "Why can't you just wear jeans to go out?" I get that, especially with younger women. She walked on the correct side of the sidewalk — all that.

Susie: She was chivalrous, in other words.

Shar: Yes.

Susie: Have you ever been with butches who don't have the manners that you describe?

Shar: Oh god, yes!

Susie: I have, too. I've been with butches who don't particularly dress well, ones who weren't chivalrous, but I would still say they were butch.

Shar: But see, I wouldn't. I think you need to aspire to be butch. But I guess I see it on a scale, so if ten is butch then you need to get past eight for me to call you butch out loud.

Susie: For me, the first requirement of butch is resistance or rebelliousness against feminine expectations. The fact that they won't dress like a girl or act like a girl doesn't mean that they know how to be generous with anybody else or that they know how to appreciate anybody else. The second requirement is that even if they don't know how to act like a girl, they know they want the girl. [*Both giggle*]

Shar: I've insulted a few people who were talking about their butch selves by saying, "You wish." To be a good butch, you need to have manners. You need to respect the position that you're taking and polish yourself up. Learn how to do these things, learn how to pick the wine, be on time....

Susie: [*Laughing*] What is this thing with being on time? Are butches on time and femmes aren't?

Shar: Exactly. One of the nicest dates I ever had was with a fortysomething butch. She showed up at my house, and I was literally half-dressed. I had one stocking on and one off. We had an eight o'clock reservation at a nice restaurant, and I was running late. It was our first date, and I was younger and already feeling nervous. As we arrived, I whispered, "Do you think they'll be mad at us?" and she patted my hand and said, "Don't worry honey, I made the reservations for eight-thirty."

Susie: Oooh, that's so cute!

Shar: That was great.... I've also had butches who were so rude. My butch friend Andrea wants to write a Mr. Manners book because she just thinks these younger butches —

Susie: OK, here's the deal. This must be said! I don't think you are simply butch or femme. I think it's something you grow into in your lesbianness. Every butch on the planet didn't just roll out of her egg with the doctor saying, "Hey, you're a butch."

Shar: That's what I was saying about aspiring to be butch.

Susie: Everybody's a baby. These eighteen-year-olds will tell me, "I'm not butch," or "I'm not femme," and I say, "How the fuck would *you* know? You've only been screwing for three years." [*Shar laughs*] This is something you grow into. It's not going to be handed to you, and it's not going to happen overnight. Sometimes it's not even predictable — I know some people who said that it was like menopause — they transformed.

If Emily was your first butch lover, did you know what was coming? Did you know that she would be different?

Shar: I didn't know how nice it would be, no, and that I would feel so relaxed with it. We met at one of your book signings. Remember? I had already noticed her — she came swaggering through the audience to sit right in front. Your topic was butch/femme and the dilemma of lazy femme bottoms. I had responded from the audience, "Your butch friends haven't met the right femmes." Afterwards, she came up to me and said, "I want to talk to you." I was looking very pretty that day.

Susie: Had you wanted to go out with butch women before, or did you think they were the icky side of lesbianism?

Shar: I knew I liked opposites — not femmes. Sometimes they were jock types, sweaty types. I always aspired to the crème de la femme; Audrey Hepburn and those early 1960s women with the long straight skirts.

Susie: I'm changing with age. I can't look like the idols of my twenties anymore. My femme qualities are changing. I've never received so much butch attention in my life as when I was pregnant. I realized that a certain kind of mom, a femme mom, was this ultra femme dimension that my dyke colleagues had not discussed before because my friends weren't mothers. Even butches who hadn't given me the time of day for years wanted me when I was pregnant.

The times I feel the most queer is when I'm in public with a butch woman because it is just absolutely clear to the straight world that you're lovers when you're dressed as a butch/femme couple. It's the closest that lesbians come to being blatant. I know these bald girls think they are making a statement, but anybody can shave her head. It could mean anything, but a butch/femme couple only means one thing. Everybody knows that they are fucking each other and they're queer. I got more recognition as a femme with a butch lover than I ever got wearing a porridge-bowl haircut and a women's symbol around my neck, which, for a time, was radical.

A lot of people come out as baby butches just to let the world know that they are dykes. You don't want to be a frilly girl, and you don't want to be a straight girl. So socially, it is set up that you come out in this baby-butch way, and then you find out if it suits you. My first butch lover took me from my baby-butch persona to being femme.

Shar: There are people who would argue with you and say that you are talking about androgyny.

Susie: But it wasn't androgyny! I was taking shop and car repair classes!

Shar: Oh, my.

Susie: I thought I was raised crippled because I was such a sissy. I signed up for shop, I tried to change my clothes to be tougher....

Shar: Would you have called it butch? Wouldn't you have defended it and said, "Why do these things only belong to men? They aren't innately masculine or feminine things." It's just something that women need to know how to do.

Susie: Yes, at that time that's what I would have said.

Shar: Well, times haven't changed. If you could go talk to those androdykes down at Café San Marcos or wherever they hang out, they would all say, "I'm not butch or femme." First of all, if I decide to call you butch, it's a fucking *compliment*.

Susie: I feel like saying, "Of course you're not! You haven't a clue... maybe if you sit in this bar long enough you'll find out." [*Laughter*]

Shar: Like Chicken Little, it will hit you....

Susie: The butch/femme sky will open! [*More laughter*] It's funny that you think of Emily as your first butch date — because I ran into butches in high school.

Shar: When did you know that they were butch dykes?

Susie: There were rumors floating around that the gym teacher was queer. The girls who hung around her were the kind of girls who would run across an entire football field to catch a ball while I was picking my nose. They were not pretty; they didn't know how to dress like a girl would dress. They upset me because I thought they missed some key developmental link. I was like, "Hey, did anybody clue you in... that you're a *girl*?" While everybody else was asking if they could borrow each other's birth control pills in the locker room, these girls were on another planet. This was about a month before I got introduced to the lesbian feminist movement. Within a matter of weeks they would become something cool to me.

A month later I went to a meeting to hear Jeanne Cordova, the editor of *Lesbian Tide*, and there I met all these hip, sexy dykes. That was my introduction, in the early '70s, to the lesbian activist milieu of Los Angeles. Then into my life came Bonnie Randler.

Bonnie Randler was a really attractive young woman who sat next to me in class, and she was *the* last word in lesbian feminism at sixteen years old! I was not her type at all. We looked sort of like each other — fresh-faced, clean, Irish — but she liked heavy breasted, tiny, intense Jewish girls with dark skin who took a lot of drugs and weren't politically active at all! Finally one day, after we both had dropped out of high school, we ended up in bed at her apartment in Venice. That Spinner's song "For the Love of You" was playing over and over again. It was finally happening. And for her being Miss Smarty Pants — putting me down for being so innocent — all of a sudden she was quite shy about taking her clothes off, about doing anything. And she wasn't the first girl I'd made love to, but she was the first *dyke*. I had fucked all my girlfriends at this point. I pushed her back to get on her to kiss her, rub on her, eat her... I don't know, *something*, and she just shrieked! She pushed me off and said, "No, no you can't. I don't come." I said "What?" She said, "Now you know! I'm butch."

Shar: NO!

Susie: She said it just like that. I had never heard anybody use that word before. In terms of what we were doing butch meant, "Don't touch me." In my very 1974, feminist-egalitarian, circular-waterbed frame of mind, I thought that was the most ridiculous, fucked-up thing I'd ever heard. If you would have asked me then what I thought of butch/femme, I would have told you that's what queers in the '50s who didn't know what to do with a woman did with each other.

Shar: That's what I would say when people would ask me if my girlfriend and I were butch and femme because I wore skirts and she didn't. I would proceed to deliver a mini queer history lesson, "No, that's what queers did in the '50s, butch/femme blah blah blah," like it didn't exist anymore. Just a moment in history! I would finish, "So, you're confused. That's not us."

Susie: With my lack of experience, I couldn't argue with her gospel of lesbianism. I couldn't say, "You're so full of shit! You're not butch. You're an inhibited little teenager who's never had an orgasm before. Why don't you lie back and shut up!" I never had enough nerve to do that.

Shar: It's interesting when you talk about high school because I consider Emily my first butch, but Karen H. was really the first butch I experienced. She took care of me all throughout high school. Karen, first of all, saved my butt from being beat up several times by the drugged-up, dropped-out, heavy metalers who hated my big-mouthed, skinny little punk ass. I wore my red rubber pumps, and outrageous clothes — this was the '80s in a small, conservative, follow-the-rules town. Then, in PE, I would stand beside her and make her laugh, and in exchange she would catch all the balls — which in my mind meant she didn't let any balls *hit me*. I would scream and hit the lawn while she would stick up one hand and catch it. Now, she's this private eye, detective, bodybuilder person.

Susie: She's gay?

Shar: Yes. I don't know if she has all the butch manners or if she's a top, because we never had sex, although we did have this sexual relationship going on based on how we played the butch/femme roles. She thought I was the prettiest little thing; she laughed at my jokes; I could do no wrong.

Susie: Part of butch/femme is the mutual appreciation society, and if you don't appreciate it then you don't get it. The thing that was really missing with Bonnie was that she never appreciated my femininity. I don't think I went out with another butch for a long time. I went out with other girls who turned out to be butches. Sometimes I feel that I got really ripped off. I did Susie Bright's coming out school for *les jeune filles*. They weren't butch with me, but they would go on to have these incredible careers with other femmes. I broke them into the anatomy lesson, and then they went on to someone else.

Shar: I'm laughing because I relate to this. I recently dated a baby butch, and I was her first femme, and considering the kind of femme I am, I guess I was pretty overwhelming. She acted like it was just a persona she was trying out. Then she went on to get completely smitten with another femme. She found me and thanked me for teaching her the joys of femmes!

Susie: [*Laughs*] That's rare!

Shar: My girlfriend told her, "Welcome to paradise!"

Susie: Let's talk about the prejudices – I always get asked, "What's different about the butchness of a woman from the masculinity of a man?"

Shar: Obviously, I get the nicer sides of masculinity with butch women without the things that come with a man. Would you say, as a bisexual woman, that you go for men who have the more feminine qualities that you like, and obviously, the inherent masculinity, and with women it would be the opposite?

Susie: For me, being femme is tied up with my bisexuality. I'm a femme before I'm anything else. I respond to certain qualities in men and women that get my pheromones huffing and puffing. I can tell you a litmus test for this that will show how truly kinked out I am.

When I first came to San Francisco, I had the biggest hots for this woman. She dressed in black with cowboy boots before that was done to death, wild eyes, one of those dangerous butches. About ten years after we met, she started going through a sex change, and she wanted to talk to me the first day of her hormone treatment. I was honored that she would tell me, yet I was upset, too, and I didn't know why I was upset. When I showed up at the bar, Angie, now Mitch, came out of the bathroom, and in this stage of his treatment he looked like a very soft, effeminate man. All the desire I had for that curvy, wicked, dangerous butch in cowboy boots went right out the window. I had no attraction at all. This proves my point – if someone asks my type, I'm a sucker for a James Dean. It's not that I don't have sex with or like other things but this is my type.

As we sat there talking I said, "I have to ask one dumb question, but I just have to hear you tell me. There's always going to be a part of me that's going to feel like you decided to do something this drastic because you couldn't find the kind of femme you deserved who would appreciate your masculinity – and that if you'd found the right femme who loved your cock, and treated you in the manner that you wanted to be treated, you wouldn't have gone under the knife." And to my amazement he said, "Oh my god, I never thought of that."

Shar: Oh my god!

Susie: Holy shit. He said he'd only been with one woman who had treated him the way that he wanted to be treated.

Butchness, for me, is a form of transgender on a continuum that is as wide as the heterosexual/homosexual continuum. I think butches are feeling a lot of traditionally masculine erotic feelings, with this sense of erotic identity that's very powerful to them because it is focused on other women. They stand out because what they're doing is so unconventional. My desires are not so easily detected in a crowd except when I'm with a woman, but I could be turned on to those desires in anybody. It would be easy to say that I've had relationships with butch women because I get all the sexy part of masculinity without the oppression of dealing with a real man. But it's not that easy. I've found that my love and my lust are never that rational. Some of the men I've been with have rejected the notion of male superiority and some of them thought it was their god-given right. With women you never have that power struggle over what you're born with. That's significant about a lesbian relationship. It's a benefit, although we had power struggles over other things, some of which were masculine traits that I didn't like.

The classic "I don't come." Now that is a lesbian thing! Guys always come. Butches withholding orgasm is a lesbian thing. But withholding feelings and being quiet about stuff and not being so socially dexterous is something that I find both attractive and frustrating no matter who exhibits it. I know I just said a million things....

Shar: It's so funny that I've had to explain to butch women that it was OK to want me in ways that are considered sexist. The young ones are butch on the outside — and when it comes down to sex, they still want to fuck you 'til your brains explode.... Right?

Susie: Right.

Shar: ...they want to have their cocks and they want to fuck you. But they don't know that it's OK for me to be on all fours saying, "We can live in a porn movie — let's go! Call me a bitch. Objectify me!" [*Laughter*] They finally get reassured, and once again I feel like I'm doing butch training. "Now you've graduated! Now you know that you can want somebody and still have power, because what I need is to be the object of your desire." I like women who enjoy possessing me in certain ways. Like putting her hand on my ass in public — some people think that's sexist, but to me it is a way of sexually and physically possessing me, or taking me into her care, that rocks my world.

Susie: I think that many PC dykes who criticize this thing because they think it's sexist, or because they think butch women are acting just like men, have no idea how much contemporary men are totally out of touch with the sexy side of masculinity. Straight white men have just left their sexuality by the roadside and gone on their way to make a lot of money while they bitch about whether or not a woman will be offended by opening a door for her. How many of them have opened a door for anybody lately?

Shar: They just want something to sit around and bitch about.

Susie: Bitch and get serviced, that's the typical thing. If there's one difference between a butch and a typical man, it's that the butch works her tail off. Butches are extremely romantic. They get so much pleasure out of the erotic tension between butch and femme. It's exciting for a femme to give herself to her. And for her to feel a femme's nurturing and possessive qualities. To feel attractive and desirable... all that stuff is really special to a butch woman because she was never brought up to know that she deserved that or could have it, whereas men take that for granted.

Shar: I remember a conversation I had with Honey Lee [Cottrell] once…. I was breaking up with a woman who was getting upset over my becoming more and more visible on the lesbian scene. I said to Honey Lee, "I feel like I have this woman's butch identity in my back pocket." I thought Honey was going to say, "You femmes think the whole world revolves around you." Instead she goes, "You *feel* like you own her identity, you *do*." She said, "That's why she's holding on to you so bad, because you're a part of her butch identity." She will always be butch; she's been a tomboy, yes, she's climbed her trees, but she doesn't feel the power of her masculinity until she's with a femme. There's a part that's lost or on hold.

Susie: I totally agree. I don't exist as a femme in a vacuum and neither does she as a butch. We can sit on the toilet or masturbate or be lonely and be a butch or be a femme, but it doesn't snap, crackle, and pop — it doesn't happen until we're together. I feel it operates on resistance. It operates by resisting the straight world; it operates in the femme's resisting men's attraction to her. Part of what makes the femme attractive to her butch is that she's attractive to straight men, yet she keeps resisting straight men and standing by her butch.

Shar: I just *love* butches who love that! Butches who are like, "Yeah, buddy, she's hot and she's on my arm, so eat your heart out!"

Susie: [*Laughs*] Again, that's a butch who's identified as a butch and understands that men are her competition and that she's got a considerable handicap, but she's also got a secret weapon.

Shar: Handicap, but she's got the girl so she's won the race. That's the thing that rocks their world.

Susie: It drives their egos right into overdrive. All those things that people are so busy saying are so sick and so developmentally screwed… Let's talk about sex… explicitly.

Shar: Us, talk about sex? Twist my arm.

Susie: Did it come as a surprise when you realized that a butch could be a bottom?

Shar: I used to preach to people about the difference between top and bottom and butch and femme, and I've been a top in a lot of circumstances. But when I was with my first butch *bottom*, like bottom of the bottoms, I thought, "Oh god, get out of my bed, I'm bored to tears!" Yet I also learned through dating some stone butches that as much as I enjoy being their fantasy and enjoy what we do in bed, I really do have to be able to fuck somebody. That's my own thing. It's been my experience that the relationship goes down the tubes unless a woman can put herself in a vulnerable position for me — I don't mean I crawl on top of her and fuck her brains out, I just mean putting my fingers inside her, licking her, having her be able to come in front of me.

Susie: That's one inequality in a relationship that is hard to deal with over time. For some reason I have the number seventy-five in my head. I'm a bottom seventy-five percent of the time. But if I don't get my quarter time of being the one who fucks, who parts *her* legs, who makes *her* bend to me in that really aggressive way, then I get really bent out of shape. I've had a lot of butch lovers whose orgasms are in a large part triggered by my coming. I have to come first or they're not going to come. Of course, I would like to have that little thrill myself sometimes. Maybe if I were multiorgasmic I could come, then they could come, then I could come.... Maybe that would be it. There's something about being the one to give it up first. Sometimes that pressure really bugs me.

Shar: Oh, see, it doesn't me.

Susie: You always like to be first?

Shar: Mostly, yeah, because first of all... I can come pretty easily when I'm excited. I get so excited from fucking her and by watching her get excited that I just have to crawl up on her face and come *now*. I don't care if she's come yet because I can't wait! So if I go first then we're all satisfied. And second of all, then I'm relaxed and can really concentrate on pleasing her.

Susie: I love the way a butch makes me feel like her pleasure is in turning me on, getting me wet, and getting me off. Like she just wants to live in my asshole or my pussy forever. That I may be impatient with my own orgasm, but she's not. This may be just a good lover rather than just a butch thing, but when she has a handle on my pussy, when she knows it really, then I belong to her. She just knows me inside and out, and it's very romantic.

Shar: In and out of bed, one butch/femme dynamic I like is how she gets proud of being with her girl. She grew up, pulled the girls' pigtails on the playground, or had crushes on teachers, whatever, then it starts. She realizes that liking girls isn't OK. She comes out, then she comes out as butch, and it's not OK, then it *is* OK and finally she just gets back to, "I want a girl and I can't believe it —

Look, I've got my girl!" Regarding sex, she's got her in bed — it's not a pubescent fantasy anymore. And I've got mine, too, but that's another subject. It's that excitement that can make the difference between fingers being good, and electricity coming out of her fingers or her dick.

Susie: Well, when a butch uses a dildo with you — for one, she usually had cock fantasies, so she would have imagined doing that before. The first person who got fucked by me with a dildo probably felt like she was in some kind of anthropological experiment with a teenager, because I kept laughing.

Shar: I was just horrible at it.

Susie: I was bad.

Shar: I was so bad.

Susie: It never occurred to me to have something between my legs.

Shar: Did you put it in the wrong place? My center of gravity was so off — I wanted it stemming out from *my* erotic center. It didn't go where I thought it should go. I had to move it up on my pubic bone. I knew I was going to be bad, but I was horrible.

Susie: Well, I felt like a little girl trying on mommy's high heels and walking around the room; that's a femme analogy, but I just didn't know what I was doing. It's not like rolling off a log to me.

Shar: I've gotten pretty good at it now but... I can dance well, it's just a completely different pelvis that moves that thing.

Susie: Everyone at Good Vibrations was teasing me, saying that the Thigh Harness was for femmes. I thought, "Screw you!" but it is! Because it mounts on your thigh, which we're accustomed to rubbing. If I could have started with that I'm sure I would have been better.

Shar: Have you ever been in bed with someone and realized that someone you thought was butch needed to grow a little more or was changing and becoming more like you?

Susie: Yes, that's disappointing sexually, but sometimes in terms of friendship it can be nice. If you end up in the role of teacher you can bond, or sometimes an argument can ensue. I think some women have cultivated a butch persona in order to hide their sexuality. Being butch for them hides their femininity, denies their orgasmic stuff. It's a way to stay a little distant from sex, to stay invulnerable, and that's not the same as being butch. Even with a stone butch — she may not hand you her orgasm, but she gives you something emotionally. There are a lot of girls running around calling themselves butch who don't want to give anything up. Their saying they are butch is more like saying, "I'm a brick."

Shar: I become more femme on the outside if I'm secure in a relationship with a butch. That's why I was able to come out as a femme in my early twenties, because even though my lover wasn't butch, she loved me no matter how I was dressing. I know that I would have toned it down or assimilated more if that's what would have been necessary to mate. It was interesting how many women in the Midwest would assume that I was dumb, that femme meant bimbo.

Susie: I get scared of butches who say things like, "I'm glad I'm a butch because femmes are so dumb or so manipulative." That's internal butch/femme sexism. Somebody I had admired was just recently quoted as saying that she decided to be butch because she could see that femmes in the lesbian community got treated the way straight women get treated by men.

First of all, I want to say, hey baby, you don't just *decide* — it's not so cut and dried. Second of all, it's so disrespectful of your womanhood to say that we're the dishrags of lesbian relationships.

Shar: I was assumed to be stupid in a political way. Women didn't know whether I was blindly following the system or whether I was purposefully buying into the patriarchy and was thus a traitor, back-stabbing my sisters. For some people, a pair of high heels can only mean those two choices. They don't see the other choices, the power.

Susie: Many butches have resentments against femmes, mostly because they don't get the sex they want and are so giving — give, give, give. "I licked her pussy and gave her a diamond ring, and then she left me for a guy (or another woman), and she didn't give me what I wanted." I just want to talk to the femme in those circumstances because I can just see how claustrophobic she felt with this butch trying to buy her love or demonstrate her codependence and love every second and not give her any room to breathe. If that butch wanted to get her clit licked and have big orgasms, why didn't she say so instead pushing the femme away?

Shar: You go, girl!

Susie: OK, here's my number one criticism of butches in bed.

Shar: Go ahead. You know, you're saying my life out loud.

Susie: [*Laughing*] As a femme, when someone makes love to you, and you want them to touch you a certain way, or you want them to stop doing something because it hurts —

Shar: Oh, go on, go on, go on!

Susie: When you're femme, and you're trying to get your way in bed, you do so by making little moans and mews and moving your body a certain way....

Shar: Wiggling...

Susie: *Lots* of wiggling, and if she is doing something you don't like, you very sexily wiggle into a new position or do something incredibly seductive to lead her down a different path, right?

Shar: Exactly.

Susie: Because we're such brilliant little manipulators, right? [*Laughter*] And you would never, ever, want to hurt her feelings or her ego by slowing down this little locomotive that's inside her. It is always a bit of a crap shoot with a new lover. So, you're down there trying to figure *her* out — you know, walking through the Yellow Pages, licking, touching, stroking, doing whatever, trying to do your best to be grounded, to be intuitive to what she wants. And so many times I've been just stopped dead in my tracks by some butch putting her hand out to stop me, just saying, "No, I don't like that," or "Stop, you're not doing it right." Well, that's direct. So when that happens it's hard for me, as it would be hard for her, to just keep on trucking. She's not wiggling, she's not giving...

Shar: It's a nightmare!

Susie: It's really hard on the femme ego — especially for a femme who's usually on her back, and is probably already feeling a little insecure about how well she can fuck a butch — to get these one-word negatives and firm hands stopping her. It makes you want to say, "OK, do me. Let's go back to what's easy — me directing you, giving you all the cues so you know just what to do." I've worked through this in a long relationship where I said, "You told me you wanted it to be magic — how your last girlfriend (the really wonderful femme) knew just what to do. Well, she had some luck or something. It's not because I'm that bad in bed. You can't just tell me that you're going to say 'no' and that I should have the balls to just keep on trying. I'm a human being and anybody would be hurt by this."

Shar: I started out laughing, but as you progressed I became more amazed because you just described my experiences to the letter. It is amazing that they are this common.

Susie: My friend Jill says that the bottom line on butch/femme is who fucks and who gets fucked, in the sex sense. If you feel really comfortable giving or getting in one of those ways, then that's your comfort zone. It's difficult to learn the other way. It's taken a lot of insight to get past someone's superficial protest and just keep pushing ahead. It's always easier for me to open up and to give. It's harder for my butch lovers to give to me like that, that "open your legs and show me your pussy and just give it to me" kind of way. I feel so powerful when I open my legs for someone. It's much harder for butches to access that kind of power. When they do, then they usually want to get married!

Shar: I've never worked through this with one person. I've learned how to deal with someone's pussy in a very submissive way. Also, I've been with women where I've had my fingers in them or whatever but had to be still to let them get into their fantasy world, which is hard, especially if I am getting turned on, because then I want to wiggle or ride their thigh. It's a special trick to get them to feel comfortable enough to give it up to you without you completely taking their power away.

Susie: Yeah, if you try to fuck a butch like a girl you'll humiliate her. At the same time, if I'm going to respect her butchness while I'm fucking her, she better not make me feel like some bumbling guy who doesn't know what he's doing or like a butch failure because I'm not a butch, and I'm not a failure.

•

The Men in My Life

An Interview with Lou

LILY BURANA

LOU *is a New York-born and raised leather dyke who moved to San Francisco in 1989. As a butch dyke and S/M player who occasionally adopts a "daddy" persona, it's no surprise that Lou should have much to say about the influence of the men who've figured prominently in her life.*

Lily Burana: Now, how would you define your relationship with Rusty?

Lou: Well, Rusty is my poppa. I think of him as p-o-p-p-a, poppa, and his boy, Michael, is my nasty, evil, wicked stepmother. Rusty was the first male I met when I moved to San Francisco. I took the motorcycle skills course about a month after I got here, and he was in the class, and he was, you know, this little, adorable — not little — but adorable, redheaded faggot. When the course was over we went for a ride, and one night we went out together. We went out to the old Lone Star before the earthquake, before it went down, and we also went to the Eagle. It was that night I said, you know, "I'm going to dress to pass." He totally didn't get it. "You dress anyway you want, darlin'." So I dressed in my leather pants and a tight tee-shirt and a shirt over it and my leather jacket and a cap. I didn't pack because the Lone Star was a men's bar. I didn't know if the guys would think I was a guy or a girl or get insulted or what. So I didn't pack. But we went down there in his van, and we were about to walk in there, and I had this image of getting carded and them figuring out I was a girl. And he goes, "You look like a boy, darlin'. I'm going to introduce you as Lou to my friends." And that was where Lou was born, that very night. So we went in there and he introduced me as Lou and we got a couple of Budweisers and had a couple cigars, and we leaned up against the wall and talked, and he was like, "You just got cruised."

Lily: By a guy, by a faggot.

Lou: By a guy, by a faggot. And he was like, "Goddammit, you just got cruised again." So anyway we had a good time with that.

Lily: You big chicken. That's why.

Lou: Yeah, I was a chicken, a butch chicken. Anyway, it was a great bar because the men were so affectionate with each other. It was one of the first places I'd really seen men just putting an arm around each other and just kissing and being really friendly and no attitude. And then we went to the Eagle and we had another Budweiser and another cigar, and I continued to get cruised as chicken, and he continued to cruise and get cruised. So we just had a very nice time, and we started hanging out together. During that period Rusty was single. He and Michael had broken up, supposedly, and of course Michael says they've been together twelve years with one year off for good behavior. But they *were* single for about a year, and so Rusty and I had a lot of time to ride. We both cruised and whatever, but we had a lot of time to establish our relationship before Michael and he got back together. Because they're very married, and they don't go out a lot, and I think if they had been together we probably would never have gotten together. So that's how I met Rusty.

Lily: What's the dynamic of your relationship?

Lou: Well, he's a gay leather faggot top man, fist top, basically, and I am a dyke, and I also identify as a gay leather top man who happens to be into girls. And our relationship is not sexual by nature. There is no sexual attraction there. There's a great deal of affection. There's a great deal of love. There's a great deal of laughing and amusement. But in some ways he's sort of like a mentor. I mean, he really encourages me not to put up with a lot of bullshit, and he's the only one who calls me his little girl. He calls me "baby doll." And it's really a friendship. It feels like a lot of very, you know, unconditional love on his part.

Lily: What do you get out of the relationship with him that you wouldn't get out of a relationship with, say, a straight man?

Lou: God! Well, for one thing, he's a gay male. My dad was a gay man, and my father died four months before I met Rusty, so I think I was really hungry for gay male companionship. And also, because my dad was a faggot, I used to read *Drummer* and various boy-boy porn, so a lot of my sexuality was very gay male-oriented. So here was a hot gay man who would bring home five or six tricks a weekend. He would always make jokes about how he was going to put a turnstile in the front hall, and all his tricks would have to pay twenty-five cents each and we'd be going to Rio from that. So he was a very hot, sexual male being, but a male where the energy goes towards other men, which is what feels safest to me, because I don't do sex with men.

Lily: Do you feel like straight men wouldn't treat you that way?

Lou: I don't know. I don't have many straight male friends.

Lily: What was your relationship with your biological father like?

Lou: Well, he was the incest perpetrator. He was also totally the star in my heavens, the sun. For a very long time I totally loved him. As a kid he was my favorite parent. My parents divorced when I was three, and my mother remarried when I was four. When I was seven, we moved to London. They lived in a big house that they rented from my aunt, and they entertained or went out every night for the three and a half years that we lived there. We had nannies, and we had a certain level of contact with them. Whereas my father, I was his only child, I was the apple of his eye, I was his darling. He was extremely physically affectionate with me. He would kiss me on the lips, he would hug me, he would hold me, he would tell me he loved me all the time. And he would spoil me, he would give me money, he would give me presents, he would take me out to dinner, he would take me to restaurants, he would buy me toys and comic books and whatever I wanted. He said he wanted a son, and I think in a lot of ways he brought me up as a son in terms of mentally going forward and being capable and intellectual and being told I could do anything I wanted.

Lily: Was your father open to your being more of a tomboy?

Lou: Sure. He was open to that. He was open to my being athletic, playing tennis, swimming, riding my bicycle. And then when I started getting to puberty, that's when things started falling apart.

Lily: You started looking more like a girl, or what?

Lou: Maybe. I also started to have a social life. When I was in ninth grade I started wanting to spend my weekends in New York with my peers rather than go out to the country with him. I think he had a hard time with that. It was during ninth grade that I felt like things really fell apart.

When I started thinking about being a lesbian, I talked to my mother and stepfather about it, and they were extremely open. The things they had to say about homosexuality in advanced cultures were very cool, especially my stepfather. I basically came out to myself and the world the fall of my sophomore year in college, so I was nineteen. I had come back to New York for the last three weeks of summer, and every time I went out to a bar I'd get dragged home, which I thought was sort of interesting, because my dad's attitude was that I was not attractive, that I had a fat ass and that I was fat and unattractive. And so I was quite surprised that these women seemed more than pleased to hang out with me and have sex with me or whatever.

I dragged out of my father that he was a faggot in June of 1981, which was right around the time I slept with a woman for the first time. I came out to him in October of 1981. The first night was OK, and we talked and we told each other we loved each other. From then on he was a total shithead about it. The first woman I ever brought home he was incredibly rude to, incredibly rude. I think he was very misogynist and very homophobic.

Lily: He was more or less closeted?

Lou: He was closeted. He was gay well before Stonewall. While he didn't consider himself gay, he considered himself a homosexual. He was acting as a gay man when he was about fourteen, fifteen, sixteen, and his mother sent him to an analyst when he was sixteen who said, "Well, do you do it for money?" And Dad said, "No." And the guy said, "Well, then it's dirty and filthy and don't do it." So this is the attitude that Dad got. He was sixteen in 1949. Stonewall didn't happen until 1969, so he was gay for twenty years before Stonewall.

His attitude about two women together was "what's nothing and nothing?" He said this, making two zeros with his hands. It was pretty unpleasant. I think one of the other challenges we had is that I'm a top and he was a bottom, and I don't think that went over very well with him, either. So things deteriorated.

Lily: What did you value most in your relationship with your father?

Lou: Well, I think my mind, my independence and my *fuck you* attitude comes from him. A lot of my gay male identification comes from him. He really did love me, and he gave me the feeling of being loved, that one can be totally loved and adored and held and made much of and just be at the center of someone's heart. He was not a perfect human being, by any means. I've learned a lot about responsibility because in a lot of ways he wasn't responsible. I got to see how my view of what was good changed over time. I still will not accept the premise that women are going to be by definition like shit, or are going to be by definition less than, or going to be by definition *whatever*. I feel like part of that comes from my dad — for although he was a misogynist, he did the very best that he could with me. He gave me a sense of my integrity and of my right to be whoever the fuck I want to be and to do whatever the fuck I want to do. If other people don't like it, too bad, they can just suck up and deal.

Lily: What about your relationship with Rusty?

Lou: What did I value most? Oh, I'd say the unconditional love is a big one. I'd say just having a really warm, loving, older, safe, nonsexualizing male around. Yeah. He's really beautiful, he's really male, he's really butch, although he definitely queens around. He just has a lot of time and space for me, and I have a lot of time and space for him. I see him as innocent and a very loving being and a very caring being. And I feed sad. Partially because I already feel sad and partially because I fear the loss of him. I'm basically putting out as much positive energy as possible in terms of his process and his life and his doing what he wants and getting what he needs.

FTM/Female-to-Male

An Interview with Mike, Eric, Billy, Sky and Shadow

DEVA

THERE *is as much mystery surrounding female-to-male transsexuality as there is surrounding butchness. Since no source of information on FTMs is more credible or insightful than FTMs themselves, we shunned speculative pieces in favor of the following round-table discussion.*

Deva: The biggest question is "why?" Why do you do pursue male physiology? What is it you *don't* get from having a butch lesbian identity, or from playing boy games as gender roles, so you want to carry your identity to the next step — transsexualism?

Mike: That's like asking "what is the meaning of life?"

Shadow: For me, there is really no other choice. I didn't belong. The dyke community's been really great, keeping me around for the last twelve years and putting up with my bullshit, but there's no other course of action for me.... I was farting around in the bathroom one day and walked past the mirror and got to thinking, "God, what do I want to look like in twenty or thirty years?" Then it hit me, "God, what will I look like as an old woman?" And I freaked out. I refuse to grow up to be an old woman. It's incongruous with what's in my mind. That was what made it real clear that I was ready to start doing this. And it's something I've been dealing with since 1980.

Mike: There's been a lot of rumors about lesbians in San Francisco either going straight or becoming men, and that's just total bullshit. It's not something that you play with and then go back. Once you start taking hormones, certain changes are going to happen that are not reversible.

For me, it was strange — I never really identified as female, but I identified as a lesbian for a while. Being a dyke gave me options. I knew I wasn't straight; I tried it, and it didn't work. I wanted to be with women. But the more I was out in the lesbian community, and the more I was out into S/M, the more I came to realize that, hey, I didn't fit there either, exactly. For me, it's not about being a man or being a woman, cuz there is some fluidity in there. I identify primarily as male, but I still have roots with the women's community that I don't want severed. I'm thankful that I was socialized female, and I'm very thankful that I have the options that I have now. But I've been told, "You can't be a man, you can't be masculine, you can't do this, you can't do that, girls don't..." And I've had to wear dresses [for] work.... I now have the option to explore my masculinity. So of course I'm going to go off and do that. In five years, who knows? I may find a common ground where I'm fifty-fifty. But right now that's not where I'm at. And I'm tired of people assuming that they know what's going on with me because of what somebody else is doing. Or — the men identify me as a woman and won't play, the women identify me as a man and try to get me the hell out of women-only space. So what am I left with?

Billy: I find that a lot of people don't take my shit seriously. They think it's play, because I'm not on testosterone now. I don't feel male, and I've never felt female. I tried — I went through the whole lesbian separatist bullshit, "I hate men, blah blah blah." It never occurred to me that I could change my gender. So a lot of this stuff is really new for me, and I want to make sure I'm doing it because I can't live in this body anymore. I want to make sure that when I start the testosterone, I'm not doing it because I feel pressured. I do other stuff — I work out, I pack, I bind [my chest], I do things that are really physically uncomfortable to me so that I can look like more of what I want to be or what I feel inside. In the dyke community, and in the leather community, people still try to pigeonhole you. I wish people would just accept me. Accept the name [change] and the energy that I put out. Which I feel is very male. I've had this problem for ten years now with women being attracted to my boyishness and my masculinity, but once they get involved with me they tell me I'm too male. They encourage me to play with this, and when I talk to them about how I feel inside, and really let my guard down with them and talk about all this shit that I felt as a kid and all the shame around this...

Deva: It crosses the line.

Billy: Yeah, it crosses the line. It's not a fad. This is a very real, very personal, very hard thing for me to deal with in my life. It's not something that's easy, that's fun, that's a game. I won't, at this point, wear facial hair. Cuz I want a real moustache. I want a real beard. I'm not content with gluing something on. I want it to come out of my face. I want it to be mine. I don't want it to fall off while I'm kissing somebody.

[*Laughter*]

Eric: The lesbian place was really good for me from thirteen to twenty. That was a place for me to be in a genetic female body and be butch — to be male. I ran into a lot of problems with being called too male, and I would try really hard not to be sexist. But then I couldn't live with the split anymore... I didn't want to go back to being *she*. I was like, "No, this isn't a game for me anymore." And I disagree, I think it *is* a fad. I have a hard time... I mean, it's nice that it's really common in terms of people talking about it, so that I'm not such a freak to people, but on the other hand I feel really uncomfortable with it being so casual. Because for me it's a very painful thing.

Shadow: I feel ripped off sometimes. It's like, people who are fucking around with it are invalidating my experience. And for some of them I'm sure it's not intentional. But some of them — their attitudes...

Billy: It's drag.

Deva: Are you talking about gender play or are you talking about taking testosterone?

Shadow: I've seen both. I mean, people who have done the testosterone — not so much here in the last few years — but people [who] have vacillated back and forth, and all of a sudden they don't want to do it anymore..."Oh, I screwed up, I didn't mean to do this, the doctors should have been more thorough in their tests, they should have stopped me from doing this...." That's bullshit. I spent ten years trying to figure out if this is what I was going to do or not.

SKY

The one thing I wanted to be very clear about was how well I knew myself before I did any of this. And people who don't take responsibility for themselves piss me off to no end. Because those of us who are serious about it end up paying for it. The doctors won't do the surgery unless you have cash up front. And we're talking not about five or six hundred dollars, we're talking anywhere from five thousand dollars for chest surgery to fifteen and thirty thousand dollars for a hysterectomy, and beyond that for the phalloplasties. It has a snowball effect. And gender is the issue of the nineties. It all of a sudden sparked in the late eighties, and now everyone's talking about it and doing it.

Mike: It's like anything else. For a while, blood sports were the big thing. And for a while, fisting was the big thing. And then, gender and cigars and moustaches were the big thing. I take a contrary view to Shadow. I don't feel invalidated. I feel that anyone who wants to play with it and explore it in any way, shape or form they want to — fine. Those people who are serious, and it's part of their

On the photo: CATHY OPIE

life, will either continue to crossdress and play with gender or will come to the realization — if they are FTM — to deal with that. I think the people who really fuck us over are those people who start the process and then put it off on somebody else. I mean, if you make the conscious decision to go forward, you are responsible for making that decision.

Sky: Part of the problem that *I* have is clearly exhibited by the group of us gathered here. I think I can safely say that everyone except me is very, very male-identified. My dysphoria has to do with my physical body, and not my emotional self. Everybody else in this room is physically much more androgynous than I am. I clearly have very "girl," curvy body parts, and always have. My dysphoria has to do with my body not being the body that lives inside of my head. I get a little annoyed — a lot annoyed — about this process having to be one way. About everyone's assumption that if you start this, "this" is the end result. Because it's different for all of us.

I am striving to be what I really believe lives inside me, and that's a shape-shifter individual. That's an individual who can walk in many different kinds of worlds. That masculine person who has lived inside of me never got validity because I have 38DD tits. No matter what I do, I have those. Even when I would bind, even when I would do those things, there are certain physical characteristics that come [only] by using the drugs — the squaring of the jaw, the typical male receding hairline at the temples, the voice — unless you're fortunate enough to have that.

We all have individual reasons for doing all the stuff we do in our lives. For one of us to say, "What you're doing isn't OK because it's not what should happen," is just as absurd as people putting that crap on us when we were in the dyke community. My emotional affinities are still very clearly with queer women. I'm forty years old, and I've been involved with dykes for more than half of my life. I'm not going to give that up. That's where I feel good. I don't particularly feel good about certain individuals now who want to put their trips on me, but all in all the dyke community is home. My process is not to fully identify and realize myself as a man. But neither am I a woman.

Eric: This group is not extremely representative of FTM's…. I think I'm the only one in this room who is pretty much only into girls and pretty much straight-male identified. Although I have a lot of history in the gay community — it will always be a part of me, just as having been born female will be part of me.

Deva: I don't think this is a very homogeneous group. I do think that you are all very different, but in a sense you are all in the same community.

Billy: A pervert panel for a pervert audience.

Deva: Are most of the FTM's fag-identified or are they straight-identified? Is there shit between the people who want to see girls and the ones who play more on a fag level? What are all the inter-dynamics in the community?

Sky: Up until the time when this particular group of people got involved with the FTM group here in San Francisco, it was all very non-pervert, all very heterosexualized.

Shadow: Except for Lou, who was one of the guys who ran the FTM organization. [He] was gay, and had a male lover, but he was the only one.

Billy: Part of it too was that if [the doctors] knew that you were going to change and be homosexual they wouldn't do it. So Lou Sullivan was a real pioneer in that.

Eric: They didn't get it that gender identity and sexuality were two totally different things.

Billy: When I started going to FTM groups, there were other leather-S/M people, but prior to that…

Eric: There still are people who are freaked out. There are a lot of FTM's who have gone and who have not come back. There is now a specifically straight-identified female-to-male group in San Jose. We all have to figure out what works and where it feels comfortable for us.

Mike: I've noticed that the FTM group that meets in San Francisco is fairly diverse. Some are gay identified, some identify as perverts, some identify as straight. There haven't been any major politics, but I guess if people have been uncomfortable around the pervs they haven't said anything; they have just kind of disappeared and done their own group.

* * *

Sky: I think this notion of masculinity and femininity being assigned to certain genders, that's so much total bullshit. There are lots of masculine women. I had a lot of masculine tendencies. I was too extreme, I was too male, I was too this, I was too that — you know, all of those behaviors that were assigned to men that women could not have. So all those sorts of butch identity things that I had in the past, I still have. They haven't gone anywhere; it's the physical body that didn't match what lived in my brain or what lived in my heart.

Mike: Yeah, definitely.

Billy: If I could look in a mirror and not see my body between my belly button and my knees, I would like that a lot because I like the way my upper body looks. If I could just have slimmer hips and just have that male body that I have wanted and have seen on myself all of my life, that would make all the difference.

Shadow: Yeah, I've never worn shorts before. I hated the way my legs looked. Now I love wearing shorts. My legs look great; they look how they're supposed to look.

Sky: People are given drugs in this society to correct problems. You have cancer, you take this drug; you have diabetes, you take insulin, and that's what I see this as being, personally. I am taking medicine. I am taking a drug that will correct this particular problem. I am never going to be a man, plain and simple. The only part of my body that I'm interested in getting rid of, and this really has little or nothing to do with what I see as my gender, are my tits. I have not liked my tits since fifth grade when I got them. They don't belong on my body. I can't run, I can't lift weights, I can't do lots of things cuz they get in the way. I'm not interested in altering the lower part of my body at all. It works just fine; I like the parts that I have.

Deva: I think that that's a major question that people have. Do you use your pussies? Do you still like to get fucked in your pussies? Are you going to redirect that energy into some other place? Is it something you never really felt comfortable with before?

Eric: All of us are so different around this. I have never been into penetration, and I have always thought that my dick was not big enough, you know, thank god for dildoes. But still, sex is very hard for me. *Eek*. It's just a constant reminder.... I have never felt that that part of it was me; it was not right.

Billy: This is really interesting because up until about a month ago, I've never really been into vaginal penetration. I've just always been into ass play. I've been trying to get my lovers to do it to me for like ten years, and because I have this other hole, they always assume that that's what I want to have filled. It's just not the case for

MIKE

me, I'm anal… [*general laughter*]… in a lot of different ways. It's not that I hate that part of my body, it just doesn't feel like it quite belongs to me. It has a lot to do with how I perceive myself, and that is the part of me that makes me female. I've been packing a dildo for ten years now, off and on. I finally have one that feels comfortable to pack all the time. I like the way my clit works, and I like the way my butt works, and I don't know how much I want to fuck with that based on the types of surgery that are available right now. I'm exploring my options, and I feel real thankful that there are people close to me right now who are doing this who I can talk to. There's a great FTM community of people who will drop their drawers and show me what testosterone has done to their clits. It makes me feel like there's hope for me of feeling comfortable in my body without butchering it.

Eric: For me, I hope to get surgery. [But] it would be crazy not to fear that we are going to lose what already does work to the extent that it does.

Shadow: [With] most of the surgeries you suffer some loss of ability to orgasm or even of sexual desire.

Sky: Genetoplasty is probably our best bet at this time. That's my personal judgment.

Deva: How is that different from phalloplasty?

Shadow: They release the clitoris, which is in like an enlarged hood, and they take the labia and they enlarge them a little because most of the time with testosterone they shrink. Then they'll insert prosthetic balls, and actually create a scrotal sack out of the major labia. But you don't fuck with any of the sensation.

Sky: Phalloplasty is reconstruction from other parts of the body... like skin grafts.

Eric: The [lower] surgeries are not great for us right now.

Shadow: Not great for either direction. Male-to-females suffer the same loss as female to males do; it's just not talked about a whole lot. I have a couple of male-to-female friends who have to pee laying down in a tub because of the damage that has been done to them through their surgeries.

Mike: Surgery scares the hell out of me. I've done so many medical malpractice cases [as a lawyer] that I'm terrified. As far as I've gotten is upper surgery — I can't wait to get my chest cut. But I'm still not happy with what I've seen. Just recently I heard about this doctor in New Orleans who does a decent job so you don't have a scar going from one side of your body to the other, but until I can afford it, and until I can check this guy out, I'm not going to do anything. As long as it gets done by next year, that's good enough for me.

Sky: I'm a pig. I like to pitch and I like to catch. I am way interested in penetration in all of the available openings. I like to get fucked in the cunt and I like to get fucked in the ass, and I don't foresee that being an issue for me. It depends on what kind of modality I'm in. Oftentimes when I am doing the stiletto heels, and the seam up the back of the leg stockings and the leather skirt, I know I am downright evil and I'm just a fucking bitch, and that's exactly how I want to be treated, and that involves having my cunt fisted and whatever. When I'm doing a daddy thing, when I'm clearly in my male modality or my male-mood stuff, I don't want my cunt fucked with at all. In all circumstances, in all situations, my clit is, of course, very important. My clit or my dick, depending on how it is that I perceive my body to work that particular moment.

Deva: Knowing how hard it can be just coming out to family members about being queer, I would think it would be extremely difficult trying to explain gender issues, particularly to parents. For those of you who still maintain family ties, how has this affected your dealings with different family members?

Mike: My sister is getting married in November, and I got a card from my mother about how nice it would be if I wore a black cocktail dress to the wedding, so I was forced to come out to them. I wrote them a letter and just spilled my guts. The thing that hurt them the most was that I would think they wouldn't love me anymore. I think that I happen to be very fortunate. My mom is freaking out. My Dad... for the first time in my life I spent over an hour talking to him, and he actually said how he was feeling about stuff. It wasn't "Don't do this," or anything like that. It was, "You're old enough to make your own decision, and whatever you decide we'll stand by you, but please please please check it out and be absolutely positive before you have any surgery that this is what you want."

The thing that he said which was the hardest for me to deal with was, "You have a black parent and a white parent, and you're a mixed breed. The blacks don't like you cuz you're white, and the whites don't like you cuz you're black. You're doing this in terms of your gender, how are you ever gonna find a partner? How are you ever going to be happy?" Well in the middle of my father saying this, I've been having trouble finding dates. So how can I argue with the man when he's absolutely one hundred percent correct? All I know is that in order for me to have peace of mind, this is what I have to do.

Billy: I'm not out to my family about this yet because it is pretty recent for me. I'll do it when it feels right. At this point I'm not ready to deal with their shit. I remember coming out to them about being gay, and it was a really big deal.

Sky: I hadn't talked to my family in about a year and a half, and then I talked to my parents on Mother's Day. And in a kind of nonchalant way, came out to them about what was going on. My mother figured it out very quickly when I said, "Hi Mom," and she said, "Who is this?" Of course, [over] a year and a half, my voice had changed significantly. My family has gotten very used to the fact that I am really different than they are, *really* different. And so this came as no big shock to them.

[I spent] most of my life being my father's favorite son. There was never any "you're a girl and you can't do this," because it was just a survival tactic, learning what you needed to learn in order to get by in the world. I learned how to cook and sew from my mother, I learned how to fix cars from my father, and so it was pretty normal, and I lived my life that way. I had a kid eighteen years ago, did not have the benefit of marriage, [and] not a big trip was put on that except for about two seconds, and then my mother went out and spread the news to the entire world that she was going to be a grandmother, and she was very happy. So when I told them about this, my mother thought about it for a second, and her only concern was – was I OK, did I have friends, did people still like me. She told me, "I know that you have always done things differently in your life, and I haven't always agreed with them, but as long as you're happy and it works for you, that's what's important to me. I won't worry about you."

Deva: How about your daughter?

Sky: No parent could ever ask for a more loyal, more loving child. I had occasion to go on TV not too very long ago, and she went on the television with me to talk about what this was for her, to have this person who gave birth to her suddenly make this transition. Poppy got up on the television and said, "You know, my mother has always been both of those people to me. My mother raised me alone. She went out and worked and supported me, and did those things that a traditional father would do. She taught me things that boys know." So for her, I've always been that sort of duel parent anyway. She also knows that regardless of what I look like and what I do, I will always be her mother, and that won't change. She started to get a little panicked when she thought I would no longer be her mom, and so knowing that, she's OK. She's very solid. She defends me left and right to people who don't get it and don't understand it. She gets it to the point where on Mother's Day I get flowers, and on Father's Day I get ties.

Shadow: I just got back two or three weeks ago from seeing my parents for the first time in five years. I didn't tell them about myself, but when I started the hormones, the first time I was on the phone with my mother she says, "What's wrong with your voice?" And I said, "Well…there's an unusually high pollen count today, Mom, I'm a little hoarse here." And she was like, "Well, god, it sounds like you're on testosterone!" and I'm like, "That's funny,

Mom." Aaagh!!! My mother was a nurse for years, so she's not a dummy about this stuff.

I came out to my youngest brother, and he's cool with it. His biggest concern is similar to Mike's father's — make sure you pick the best damn surgery, make sure you know what you're doing before you go into it, and don't let them fuck you up. My mother, being a mother, finagled some of the information out of him one night, so they know. When I went down there a few weekends ago, we didn't have any time alone to sit and talk about it, but there were so many hints dropped from both directions. They would not quit going on and on about how good I looked. Before I went down I did shave. I wasn't going to slam it in their faces, but I have changed drastically physically, so it was enough of a jolt to them just in that.

What I'm working towards is setting up a phone conversation at a time when they are both home and we can sit down and talk. But that weekend was the best weekend in the past fifteen years with my father. He and I had a very difficult time when I came out to him as a dyke; he didn't speak to me for almost ten years. Now I'm just doing a little bit at a time. I have no idea how it's going to go; I'll certainly be hurt if they go away, but there's nothing I can do about that. I learned [that lesson] when I came out [as a dyke], so it will just be applied in another direction.

Eric: I just finished telling my father. I wrote him a letter. He's not happy, but he didn't yell, and that was a good thing. He turned sixty-nine yesterday, and he just keeps saying, "I'm too old for this, I don't understand, I need more time to think about it," and that's OK. He asked me some questions, I know he's worried about me, it's the same as everybody else — he doesn't want anything bad to happen to me.

Mike: It's funny because I came out to my sister before I came out to anybody, and she was real cool on the phone, and [then] I found out the next day that she had called my ex-lover to see if I was jerking her chain and playing a practical joke. She had to double-check to make sure it was for real.

Eric: That's what happened with my sister. She was so cool when I first told her. She was like, "Well, it's not that different," and I kept saying, "Well no, it kind of is, I mean, yes I've always been pretty butch and pretty male, but it *is* different." And right after that she kind of shut down. It's like once she got it, she just couldn't deal.

Deva: Whenever I have talked to friends in other parts of the country about women I know who are either playing with gender or actually taking hormones, the usual reaction is shock, cynicism, and "You San Francisco dykes!" So I wonder if FTM's outside San Francisco are more closeted, or if they are moving to more tolerant places.

Sky: I maintain the mailing list for the FTM group, and I haven't seen a big influx of people moving here. What I *have* seen are more names across the country being added to the mailing list, people trying to get information from groups that already exist. There are groups of us all over. There's certainly a lot more tolerance here — you can't have the kind of group that we have in Rapid City, South Dakota.

Deva: Is there anything else you guys want to talk about that you feel is important?

Sky: I wanted to talk just a little bit more about that particular thought, about people coming to San Francisco and this being trendy. I think that it's more of an evolution of a culture that's really starting to examine what our lives are about. We've gotten more and more defined about people who are incest survivors, people who are abuse survivors, and taking parts of our lives apart and examining them and figuring how they work and how they don't work, and how they make us be who we are. I don't see it as a trend that will be dropped; I see it as a trend that more people will follow and begin to examine how they feel about their sexual identity and their gender in the world.

Shadow: The cynical part of me doesn't believe that. I certainly hope that that's true, and I would really like to see that happen because this human race could use it. But there's also the part of me that's watching leather and S/M get very yuppified — all of a sudden it's the thing to look very bad and beautiful and nasty....

Deva: Like Madonna.

Shadow: Yeah. I mean, Harley Davidson has gone yuppie, for Christ sake.... The cynical part of me says it's a trend.

Mike: The one thing that I wanted to stress was that whether you're into genderfuck, genderblur, genderplay, whatever you want to call it, does not mean that you are FTM or will become FTM. So whoever's reading this, if you're interested in exploring it, if it feels good, do it. Ask questions, check it out, and don't be afraid that just by trying something you're totally going to catch it.

Sky: I would like to say one thing in closing. For me, I have always looked to the women of the world to be the trendsetters, to be the high aimers, to be the people who make other people look at things, make them think about them, make them feel about them. And I regard this particular process that I'm involved in to be yet another one of those things that women will be the pioneers in. Women who are in the lesbian community, women who are in the feminist community, whatever communities they are in, will begin to get a grip about this, and not only become advocates of people becoming more fully realized human beings, but will also be the pioneers in stopping this insanity of dealing with each other on a gender basis. And that will bring more humanity to us as a culture. I still have a lot of faith in women being the ones to do that.

Packing, Passing and Pissing

Mike Hernandez and Sky Renfro

Packing

DILDOES can be purchased in most large cities. Good Vibrations (1210 Valencia Street, San Francisco CA 94110; 415-974-8980) in San Francisco sells a variety of dildoes in various shapes and sizes. Write for catalogs, current prices and ordering information. Stormy Leather (1158 Howard Street, San Francisco CA 94110; 415-626-1672) also sells some of the products mentioned in this article.

From experience, we recommend the flaccid Family Jewel or the Herbie. While Doc Johnson (P.O. Box 9908, North Hollywood CA 91606) manufactures dildoes which appear similar to the Family Jewel, they have a tendency to be too hard. Feel free to experiment and exchange information within your own communities to determine what is best for you. Remember that each product has its merits and drawbacks.

The Family Jewel is a dildo molded to represent the penis and testicles. It is made up of a combination of latex and two other plastics. The Family Jewel comes in six-, seven- and nine-inch models and in Caucasian, mulatto, and black (these are the designations used by the manufacturer). If believability (passing) is the goal, the six-inch model is recommended; otherwise the bulge becomes surreal. The use of cornstarch on realistic-looking dildoes such as this one makes the texture appear less shiny and more like real skin.

The manufacturer sells this item as a novelty only and makes no warranties or representations as to any use other than as a novelty. We believe that this is due to repressive state laws.

Pros: Softer and more comfortable than the standard hard plastic or silicone dildoes. Realistic appearance. Can be packed in a jock strap or modified harness. Estimated cost: thirty to thirty-five dollars.

Cons: The balls tend to shear off because there is no hardener in the solution. They tend to be too soft for use other than packing. When first purchased there is a distinct odor of plastic which diminishes in time and with exposure to air. Packing for longer than eight hours (varies with individual use) may result in discomfort. Failure to clean regularly could result in yeast infections. As with most silicone and plastic dildoes, there may be quality control problems such as small holes where air got into the mold during the manufacturing process, or variations in color depending on the dye lot.

The Herbie is an industrial sponge hand-carved and crafted into the general shape of a penis. The Herbie comes in a variety of colors as well as the natural color of the sponge. As the product is created by hand, a variety of sizes are available. The Herbie can only be purchased through Rhon of Creative Growth Enterprises (4480 Treat Boulevard #227, Concord CA 94521; 510-798-0922). Estimated cost: forty dollars. Write for brochure.

Pros: Realistic in feel through clothing. Since the Herbie is made from sponge, it is extremely comfortable and can be packed for hours on end without any soreness or pain. Can be packed in men's briefs or a jock strap. No harness required. In some situations minor modification of the flap in the briefs are required. Easy to clean.

Cons: The only use available is packing. In other words, the Herbie does not pass if you "whip it out." The Herbie tends to get hairy. It "walks around" if not worn with snug underwear or a jock strap or if other measures to secure Herbie are not taken. It expands when wet, such as in a swimming pool, and takes a while to dry. You can remedy this by owning more than one.

We have heard of a packing device described as a prosthesis (simulated male penis) which is coated with a latex material. The prosthesis and harness are made to the purchaser's desired specifications. Write to Randy Ingersoll, 315 Running Brook, Mesquite, TX 75149.

We know that other products exist, but we do not have sufficient information to comment on the pros and cons. If you are interested in purchasing other products, we suggest that you first do your research by contacting the seller and asking questions. *Caveat emptor* (let the buyer beware).

If you have the time and inclination, you can create your own device. You can purchase sponge or a piece of industrial foam and cut or carve it to create a packing device. We know of people who have created this using scissors or dog grooming shears. Since you are spending your time, and materials are much cheaper than buying the completed product, there should not be a lot of stress about making mistakes. Who knows, your mistake could be the next improvement in the design.

Pantyhose, hair gel and condoms can create a product similar to that sold by Randy Ingersoll. Hair gel (the goopy stuff) is placed in non-lubricated condoms to form the product. For the balls, place hair gel in the condom and work it down to the tip. Once you have a sufficient space which appears oval, place the condom in another condom and tie them off. By "double bagging" you will protect your clothing and prevent leaking and staining in the event of breakage. Repeat the process with the other ball. As in nature, one ball should be slightly larger than the other. Place the two balls in knee-high pantyhose, and once situated to your satisfaction, place them in another knee-high. Use a small stitch to keep them in place. Do not perforate the condom as it will later burst and leak.

Use the same process for the penis as for the balls. Obviously you will need a lot more gel for the penis. Feel free to experiment to get the size that you desire. Do the same for the penis, and then use a running stitch or a basket stitch (or whatever works for you) to take up the excess material. Turn the knee-high inside out, and reinsert the condoms containing the penis. This should provide a nice tight tube-like section. Do not worry about how the device looks; it's how it looks and feels in your jeans that counts.

Use another small stitch to sew the balls to the dick, and it's ready to use. If you want, you can attach elastic to create a jock-strap legging. This will ensure that the device does not move around in your underwear, and you can wear it with a jock strap, alone, or with any other type of underwear that you want to use.

We have also heard of people using Teenage Mutant Ninja Turtle

Slime. We have tried Gack, but it has a tendency to hold a shape rather than being fluid. Consequently, the bulge looks odd from time to time (especially if you are groped or adjust yourself). You can use cornstarch to develop your own consistency. This is probably the most cost-effective method.

PISSING

INTERESTINGLY ENOUGH, this seems to be a very taboo subject for women. There seems, however, to be a very large underground engaged in this type of play. There are various ways to practice watersports safely, a subject we will not address here. As for pissing standing up, if you are looking for something guaranteed, dream on. We are unaware of any device which is sure-fire, comfortable, painless, and cost-effective. But hope springs eternal. In writing this, we assume that you want to be able to piss standing up while avoiding pissing on yourself. (For those of you who flag yellow, almost anything that you use will fulfill that need for gold.)

Rhon at Creative Enterprises has developed a device which can be used to piss through, pack, and for sexual intercourse. We do not have any information on this product other than word of mouth, but believe the estimated price to be five hundred dollars, which is too steep for the "player." There is a model sold in the neighborhood of three hundred dollars for pissing only, which in our opinion is still too steep. There have been some complaints about bladder infections, that it is unwieldy, that the product does not work all of the time, and that the reservoir requires some insertion into the vaginal canal. The reservoir is a female urinary assist device manufactured by Hollister and sold at most medical supply stores. You do not have to be a doctor or in the medical field to go into one of these stores and buy urinary assist devices. Look in your local telephone book. Remember, there is nothing to be nervous about, and you do not need to explain to anyone why you want to buy one of these devices. If you insist on needing a story, tell them that you are going camping and are looking for comfort in the woods. Sales clerks will believe almost anything plausible.

Le Funnel, touted as the device which will allow biological females to piss while standing, is bulky and uncomfortable. You can't keep it in your pants, and there is no way to store it easily, as it is made from hard plastic.

Catheterization does not allow the sensation of pissing, and there are potential health hazards (bladder infections, for instance) with prolonged use. The idea of using a bardex catheter was discussed at one point in time: It would sit in the urethra while uninflated and then be inflated when the need to urinate arose. In that fashion, the sensation of needing to piss would remain. This does not seem practical in the long run.

Hollister manufactures a variety of external catheters for both males and females as well as other urinary devices. We recently purchased a female external catheter for experimentation. Unfortunately, you have to be pretty clean-shaven to use it, and it is somewhat bulky, but it can definitely be used in the context of a scene relatively freely. It does not seem practical in the long run.

We have heard of people using the plastic tops to salsa containers, Cool Whip, and other products. You merely cut away the edges so that you have a smooth circular piece of plastic. When ready to use, you bring two of the edges together and situate the device far enough behind your urethra to catch the flow of piss. After using it, you can dry it with a piece of toilet paper and put it back in your pocket. Obviously, learning to use this will take some practice. Please be aware that the hairier you are, the harder it will be to prevent pissing on yourself.

Some women report being able to place fingers around their clitoral hood to lift the area and surrounding labia so as to redirect the flow of piss forward rather than downward. This requires that you lower your pants, but you will be facing the same direction as men who piss standing up. (Personally, if I am going to drop my pants I don't want anyone sneaking up behind me.) Again, hair plays a large role.

Baby bottle nipples and tubing work fine if you have your pants all the way down. If you try them with jeans or skivvies, good luck. We have received an excellent suggestion concerning the use of bottle nipples for baby calves or other animals, but we haven't tried it yet.

You can use the baby bottle nipple in conjunction with the top of a shampoo bottle. You need a bottle of White Rain Shampoo or any other oval-shaped, soft-sided, plastic bottle. Cut from the bottom of the bottle, at a diagonal, leaving one side longer than the other. Place the nipple in the bottle top. Attach the nipple to a piece of surgical tubing (three-eighths or five-eighths recommended), and it's ready to use. Place the longer end behind the urethra and piss away. This will also take some practice. The things that you want to be careful of are backflow and any piss left in the reservoir after you are done. If you tilt the device forward slightly after you are done pissing, you should get all of the fluid out of the reservoir. As for backflow, you will need to practice varying the speed and pressure of your piss until you find the right combination for you so that you don't over-flow and wet yourself. The connector allows you to disassemble the unit for more compact travel. It travels well in a fanny pack.

Rumor has it that there are various people in the process of developing devices that can be pissed through. The trick will be developing something that will function and pass muster at the urinals. Eric (P.O. Box 767, Guilderland, NY 12084-0767) is a source for one device. Send a self-addressed, stamped envelope and a dollar twenty-five for more information and pictures.

Until then, keep on experimenting and share the information, please!!!

If you already use the men's room, please don't be overly concerned. Many men, especially those sporting Prince Alberts, sit to piss. Most guys are piss-shy and probably have permanent marks in their shoulders from hugging the urinals. Also, men do not tend to speak to each other or look at each other in the john. Women are a lot more social and observant. Therefore, we believe that it is easier to pass as a female-to-male than as a male-to-female crossdresser. If you are going to use the men's room, use the youth angle. Most of us look like teenage boys. If you feel uncomfortable, don't do it. We must warn you that there are laws against the "wrong gender" using the restroom. Use at it at your own risk.

PASSING

THE BEST source of information on passing is Lou Sullivan's *Information for the Female-to-Male Cross Dresser and Transsexual*, which contains a variety of information about transsexuality, crossdressing, hormones, contacts, referral sources, publications and films. Order from FTM, 5337 College Avenue #142, Oakland, CA 94618.

Binders can be purchased at a variety of locations which manufacture or sell rib belts or men's garters. They come in small, medium, and large. Extra large can usually be special ordered. Some purchasers have indicated that they are rugby players and use the binder to protect their breasts. This explanation has not met further questioning, but just in case, you should be familiar with the rugby leagues in your area and their playing schedules. Others have stated that they have experienced a rib injury.

Some binders are more comfortable than others. You should avoid clasps. They tend to be more uncomfortable than Velcro. Make sure that the Velcro is vertically placed as opposed to horizontally in three strips. The use of horizontally-placed Velcro tends to result in stretching of the elastic and reduced life span of the product.

Medical supply stores tend to carry these. Hittenberger's on Market Street in downtown San Francisco is a popular location. Cost varies between thirty-five and fifty-five dollars. Other medical supply places sell similar binders.

Vests are available, but tend to be less effective for larger-breasted individuals. Refer to your local Yellow Pages under "Corsets and Girdles." Stay away from ace bandages and tape. The ace bandages slip too much and are often bulky. Too much trouble and not enough believability. Tape, while more appealing than ace bandages, restricts breathing and can be hazardous to your health.

Stormy Leather creates a latex top for binding. It looks similar to a jog bra, but is made with latex. If you are small- to medium-breasted, they will make it out of a clear latex which is not as hot or as tight as the black latex. The heavier black latex is used for larger-breasted individuals. The estimated cost is forty dollars. We recommend that you be measured so that the device works well. As with all latex products, oil or oil-based materials such as lotions will cause deterioration and ultimately the latex will tear. This is our product of choice at the present time.

Moustaches, beards, etc. can be purchased at any costume makeup or wig store. Our recommendation is San Francisco Theatrical Supply on 9th Street between Mission and Market Street, above Drama Bookstore, because of the personal assistance offered. The clerks tend to be able to field questions better than the wig stores and will help you match your hair color. They will also provide general assistance and suggestions. They carry a variety of products such as pancake makeup, stipple pencils (used for beard shadows), cosmetic sponges, etc. Stippling pencils are useful for creating a five o'clock shadow. However, the difference between real stubble and fake stubble is discernible in the light of day. Classes are also available in stage makeup, which will teach you techniques for creating your own facial hair.

It is common for facial hair to be slightly darker than head hair. Observe the men around you and notice whether their facial hair is darker or lighter. It also tends to contain a variety of different colors. In other words, someone who has brown hair may have red and black hair in their beard. In most cases, since men's faces tend to be wider, you will have to trim the moustache to custom fit your face. In addition, if passing is the goal, we recommend that you shave the "peach fuzz" off your face.

There are books on the subject of stage makeup. The most useful we have found is *Stage Makeup* by Richard Corson (Prentice Hall, 1990). This book retails for forty-seven dollars and can be purchased at your local theatrical supply store. You may also wish to check your local library.

Cost-effective suits may be purchased at most urban thrift stores. Check your local yellow pages for men's clothing stores carrying a selection of short and extra-short men's suits, blazers, slacks, and dress shirts.

Men's Wearhouse and C & R Clothiers, in San Francisco, carry short and extra short suits from time to time, but they tend to be over-priced. The Short Shop on Kearny in San Francisco is another alternative, but it can be costly depending on your tastes. Their sales tend to be good. You can expect to pay anywhere from two hundred to four hundred for a good suit (i.e. quality wool or wool blend) unless you are fortunate enough to find one at a thrift store. Thrift stores offer a variety of surprises, and if you are patient and careful in your search you will be able to find something which will pass with some minor modifications. If you don't have the time and have some money to burn, we suggest that you keep your eyes peeled for a sale at one of your local stores.

In terms of passing, you should stay away from the jeans and tee-shirt look, especially in San Francisco. There are so many visible and out dykes that often people trying to pass will be unable to. You may be able to pass in Montana in jeans and tee-shirts, but not in Northern California. We suggest that you follow a more conservative look, such as dress shirts and slacks, at least initially. Spend time going to your local mall or gay bar and watch guys. How do they walk? What are they wearing? What do their bodies look like? Once you have a sense of carriage, walk, attitude, you may be able to successfully pass in jeans and tees.

Men come in a variety of shapes and sizes, and so do we. Do not assume that you have to have no hips and big biceps to pass. It may help, but it's not a must.

Dress shoes can be purchased at Nordstrom's for a fairly reasonable price (approximately sixty-five dollars). They carry sizes six and up. A men's six is equivalent to a women's eight. For smaller shoes you will need to shop in the boys' department. Good luck!

SUPPORT GROUPS

FTM is a peer support group for female-to-male transsexuals, transgenderists, and crossdressers. The group offers support for the exploration of gender-identity issues, the male persona, and/or gender transition. This group meets on a monthly basis. We hold informational programs and support group meetings on alternate months. At the present time, meetings are held on the second Sunday of the month. Program meetings are open to all. The support group meeting is limited to FTMs and crossdressers *only*. Significant others and biological males are not allowed to attend these meetings, so that the participants can speak freely about their concerns and issues.

Our group is diverse in the most liberal sense of the word. We are of different backgrounds, sexual orientations, and sexual identities. We are multicultural and range in age from twenty to fifty. We include persons who are just beginning to examine these issues, as well as persons who have been dealing with them for years. There is no cost for membership. We publish a quarterly newsletter for which donations are requested. For further information regarding FTM please write to: FTM, 5337 College Avenue #142, Oakland, CA 94618.

The East Coast Female-to-Male Group is located in Boston, Massachusetts. For further information about the group, please contact: ECFTMG, P.O. Box 38-3033, Cambridge, MA 02138.

There are also groups in the East Bay, South Bay, and Sacramento for FTMs, crossdressers, and/or both.

For further information, please feel free to write Michael or Sky: RH Factor, 2215-R Market Street #438, San Francisco, CA 94114.

Information about creating your own products has been provided by a number of dykes, FTMs, crossdressers and other transgendered people whose identities will remain anonymous. Thank you all for providing this information so that it can be shared with others.

Girls and Picking Them Up: Cruising Tips for Butches

Notes from New York City's Own Clit Club

JULIE TOLENTINO

Compiled, made up, witnessed by Julie Tolentino and the Clit Club Crew: Michelle, Alistair, Robin, Pam, Diviana, Alice and Friends.

How Do You Sophisticatedly Sexily Intelligently Unrefusably Saunter Up to Ask an Unknown Woman to Dance?

WE'VE all sat in a dark and crowded bar and eyed a lovely creature on the other side of the room, badly wanting her, and not known what to do next. Saying "Oh, what a babe" to your buddies gets dull for all after the first fifteen minutes. Showing off your favorite rugby tackle may not impress her. But if the walls could talk at the Clit Club, they would sag, holler, buckle, and guffaw over our age-old attempts to find, enchant, mesmerize, snag, fuck, or avoid each other. We Clit Clubbers have spawned the following suggestions to help ease our butch soulmates' anxieties as they seek to fulfill that eternal and biological urge to mate.

Smoke Advice

Lighting cigarettes still seems to have its charm.

Lots of girls bum cigarettes and lights when they want to show that they care. When we offer them their own pack of matches they say, "Oh no, I just want to keep coming back over and have you light it."

One crowded night at the Clit Club, A. was squeezing through the crowd with an unlit cigarette in her hand, and a girl who'd been cruising her all night grabbed the cigarette, lit it with her own, and led the woman on her way with a devious, alluring smirk. An impressive attempt.

"Hello, Beautiful" Advice

Whenever you have a chance, say things like, "Hello, beautiful."

Cruising Is an Individual Sport

We've watched cruising butches ask the bartender, doorperson, or club manager to cruise some babe for them and send back the results. No, no, no. Cruising butches strike out by asking others to intercede. If you want to get a drink for a babe, bring it to her. If you want to ask her to dance, be sure and do it yourself. Many times we've seen that pretty girl fall for the first one to approach her. You could lose her to your messenger. First come, first serve.

Perseverance

When in doubt, persevere. One girl, courting the bartender, swore she would come to the bar every single Friday night until the bartender gave in and slept with her. She still comes every Friday.

Flirting and Eternal Flirts

Many of us meet a flirt-o-matic and fall for her without knowing she is a compulsive, irresponsible and indiscriminate flirt. How can you find out if she has one girlfriend or ten? How can you discover the skeletons in her closet? How seriously should you take her? Don't worry, have a little fun, leave your heart out of it, and don't give her your credit cards. Remember this self-defense technique: Be sure to obviously flirt with that flirt-o-matic when her girlfriend is in the room. She gets what she deserves.

P.S. The best person to ask about a person's marital status is the coatcheck girl. She knows who came with whom.

Bathroom Lines

The bathroom line isn't the best place to make a deep impression. If she's really got to go, she probably isn't paying attention.

Clean Your Fingernails

Wear clean socks and clean your fingernails. Butch hands are true sex objects.

PHYLLIS CHRISTOPHER

JULIE TORENTINO

Pool Playing and Shyness

It's OK if all you do is play pool and strut around the table. Women know how to swoop in on a pool playing studly butch. So if you want to be passive for a while, it's fine.

Sex and Holidays

Holiday nights are the best nights out. Everyone is fleeing family and relations and seeking physical relief.

If You Are Rejected

If she doesn't want you, try another one. Don't take it personally.

Approach All the Ones You Can Imagine!

If you can't choose a particular woman, approach more than one.

Clit Club Cocktail Waitresses' Definitive No-Nos

Don't pick up a pool cue, shake it into the smoky club air and say, "Hey baby, suck my dick."

Don't come into the bar with your new paddle hanging from your belt. If you lose it, you'll spend the rest of your time with a flashlight crawling on the floor. On the other hand, maybe you want to switch.

Don't try to have an intimate, personally relevant chat with a gal in front of the disco/techno/industrial/hard/slam/trance dance speaker.

Don't do splits or the polka on the dance floor.

Don't assume all couples are monogamous.

Don't assume the woman she's with is her girlfriend.

Don't assume the woman is a woman.

If you can't get it up, buy a better harness.

Try not to act stupid.

Don't act surprised if she wants to go home with you.

Don't be afraid to try.

The Essence of It All:

A favorite question, the sum of all questions ever asked at the Clit Club, the summation of all bar-going women-cruising butches of all time: A Clit Club newcomer, with wide eyes, a deep-chested sigh, and pumped-up composure, approached Alistair, our cashier, and asked, "Where do you get sex?"

When I was ages 9-12, I played with a Black Barbie whose hair was chopped off. I named her George after the butch sidekick of Nancy Drew. If I knew then what I know now, this is how I would have

BUTCHED UP BARBIE

By Vicki Jedlicka

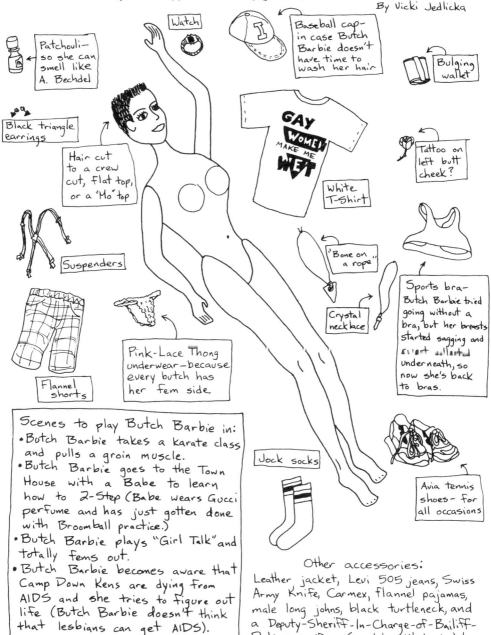

Watch

Baseball cap- in case Butch Barbie doesn't have time to wash her hair

Bulging wallet

Patchouli- so she can smell like A. Bechdel

Black triangle earrings

GAY WOMEN MAKE ME WET

White T-Shirt

Tattoo on left butt cheek?

Hair cut to a crew cut, flat top, or a "Mo" top

Suspenders

"Bone on a rope"

Sports bra- Butch Barbie tried going without a bra, but her breasts started sagging and sweat collected underneath, so now she's back to bras.

Crystal necklace

Pink-Lace Thong underwear—because every butch has her fem side

Flannel shorts

Scenes to play Butch Barbie in:
• Butch Barbie takes a karate class and pulls a groin muscle.
• Butch Barbie goes to the Town House with a Babe to learn how to 2-step (Babe wears Gucci perfume and has just gotten done with Broomball practice.)
• Butch Barbie plays "Girl Talk" and totally fems out.
• Butch Barbie becomes aware that Camp Down Kens are dying from AIDS and she tries to figure out life (Butch Barbie doesn't think that lesbians can get AIDS).

Jock socks

Avia tennis shoes- for all occasions

Other accessories:
Leather jacket, Levi 505 jeans, Swiss Army Knife, Carmex, flannel pajamas, male long johns, black turtleneck, and a Deputy-Sheriff-In-Charge-of-Bailiff-Duties uniform (complete with badge)!

That Boy

ROBIN SWEENEY

MAYBE it really couldn't work with another butch, Sam thought.

Down the hall, Jo was taking a shower. That boy worked on Saturdays, but since Sam didn't, she wasn't getting up yet. Nine-to-five trapped in the admissions office at San Francisco College didn't have many perks, but a steady pay check and free weekends were enough for Sam. Besides, she and Jo weren't seriously seeing each other — they weren't girlfriends or anything like that, as Jo had reminded her on more than one occasion — so she didn't feel compelled to get out of the mess they had made of her futon and make Jo breakfast or take a shower with her. She might go start some coffee, though.

Pulling on the first pair of boxer shorts she found, Sam stepped over the gear still scattered on the floor from last night and went into the kitchen. Her roommate, Jeff, was spending the weekend with his latest daddy, and Sam had the flat to herself. It was quieter at home when Jeff was being a boy, but much more interesting when he was topping and brought his tricks home. Living with a leather faggot was certainly different — he left the toilet seat up but didn't freak out at the noises coming from her bedroom — and so far it was working out much better than her last place, a group flat.

Communal living is always difficult, especially for a pervert, but at first it seemed like it was going to be OK. The vegetarian girls whose apartment she shared had been touchy about her leather jacket, but totally lost it one night when Jo started screaming. Sam wasn't sure if it was just the yelling or the sounds of an ass being smacked. It might have been her boychick's begging. Maybe, "Your big dick, please, Sir!" screamed at full volume had pushed them over the edge. It didn't matter what set them off, really. Sam was told at a very chilly impromptu house meeting over breakfast the next morning that she had thirty days to move out. Things with Jeff were much better, indeed.

Sam started the coffee and sat down at the kitchen table. She caught a glance of herself in the mirror over the sink and couldn't help smirking as she pushed her glasses back up her nose. Running around the house in her underwear always made her feel kind of sexy and wicked, and she liked the way she was looking this morning. Cute and solid, not fat or ugly. Nothing like a little nookie to resolve all those body-image questions. Besides, one of the very nicest things Jo had ever said to her was how much she liked big girls, and how she thought Sam was just perfect. Couldn't fight an opinion like that. Sam had a hickey on the right side of her neck that was already impressive, and her dark and shaggy flat-top was suffering from serious bedhead. It was fun having Jo around, if kind of exhausting.

Sam had decided long ago she much preferred fucking other butches. She essentially considered herself a faggot-identified dyke. Femme girls just didn't turn her on much, although she sometimes flirted with them and often admired them. She had always had a thing for other butch women, ever since her very first crush on the goalie of her soccer team in junior high school. Sam loved the way butch girls moved and the way they looked when they were being bad-asses, smoking and showing off. Sometimes Sam thought it was partly hero worship — she usually got crushes on women who were even butcher than she was, and the first several dates were usually spent figuring out who would show her soft spots first. She also liked wrestling for control, or wrestling to give up control, with someone who was just as butch and bad as Sam was. Other butches understood why Sam wanted to strap on a dick and be called "Sir." And most of the time, they understood she also wanted to get fucked herself, or be slapped around a little and called a cocksucker. And when someone who had put up with the same shit about being too obviously queer, and had learned to be stoic and a little mean

ROBIN SWEENEY

just to survive, called her name as she came on the end of her arm, it settled something inside Sam. Made it easier to feel like there was a place on the planet for her.

There was shit to deal with, of course. Sam was tired of the fight she and Jo had been having lately. As far as Sam could tell, just being fuck buddies and not girlfriends meant that Jo would never leave any of her stuff at Sam's house, causing endless arguments about who slept where and giving Jo an excuse to leave early in the morning. Sex was acceptable, but breakfast was too much like a relationship, apparently. Sam had her own intimacy issues, but she was starting to get fed up with the way things were going.

Jo was rebounding off her first serious S/M relationship, a heavy-duty mistress/property arrangement with one of the very hot femme tops in the city, and Sam probably should have expected some problems. Sam wasn't into the mistress thing herself, but she could understand why Jo had fallen for Leslie. Leslie was a big, mean motherfucker of a femme who was strong enough to pick Jo up and toss her against the wall. This was no mean feat, particularly in high heels. Jo was 5'9", five inches taller than Sam, and almost as heavy.

The first time Sam saw Jo was at a play party. There was this sexy boy, tall, tattooed and tough looking, down on the floor on her belly howling like a dog. Leslie kept telling her to howl harder as she put little holes in Jo's naked butt with her high heels. That night Leslie whipped the snot out of Jo, cut a star into her back, and fucked Jo until she cried. When Sam saw Jo come back with a stupid grin to kiss Leslie's high heels, saying, "Thank you, Mistress, thank you," Sam desperately wanted to get her hands on that boy. Sam thought it was pretty hopeless, since it looked like Jo was only into femmes, but she was willing to try. She said hello to Leslie toward the end of the party, and Leslie introduced her to Jo.

Sam heard Leslie had cut Jo loose a little while after that party. Apparently Jo had played with someone without Leslie's permission. When Leslie found out, she went to Jo's house while she was out and took back her collar. She left a note, "No excuses, little boy." Sam thought it was a little harsh, but it definitely had style.

Sam decided to track Jo down. It wasn't hard to find her. There were only a couple of bars in the city where the leather dykes hung out. Sam assumed that Jo would either be out looking for trouble or looking to get shit-faced, or both, so she wouldn't be at any of the men's bars — there wasn't a mixed event either at the One Up or the Powerplace, and it would be uncomfortable to drink yourself past your first mistress with all the leather boys cruising around you, trying to figure why someone with tits was at their bar. It was only Tuesday, so none of the floating girl clubs were happening. That left either the Cub Den or Lucky's. Sam stopped by Lucky's first, since it was closer to her corner of the Mission. They were having one of their monthly stripper contests, so Sam moved on. Besides, Lucky's was one of those loud places where you went to dance, show off a new girlfriend, or drink in celebration — not the proper atmosphere for getting over getting dumped.

The Cub Den had started out as a men's bar just off Castro Street in the early '80s, surviving as a warm-leatherette version of the heavier bars South of Market. But when all the bars and baths and backrooms started closing, the Den quietly became a women's bar. It wasn't big, but it had windows that looked out onto the street, a reasonable jukebox, and a pool table. And tonight it also had Jo.

When Sam walked in, Jo was leaning against the wall watching the pool players. Sam went to the bar, got herself a drink, sat down at the table nearest Jo and took off her gloves. Jo grunted hello.

"Don't be rude. Sit down and talk to me." Sam amazed herself. She wasn't usually this assertive, but she kept her face still until Jo, after a long moment, sat down. Sam thought that packing her dick had probably given her more balls than usual. She hoped that tonight her glasses made her look older than twenty-five and authoritative, not owlish.

The rest of the conversation was less chilly. They progressed from razzing the pool players and arguing about the jukebox to more details about Leslie. (Sam pretended not to know about Jo being dumped and was properly sympathetic.) Jo even got up to get Sam's next drink and presented it to her with reasonable grace. Sam told Jo that she was a good boy, and she looked very flustered.

After their pool game, Mike and Larry came over. In the real world, they were both paralegals at the same huge Financial District law firm, where they were Mary Ellen and Laura and wore stockings and pumps, not the cowboy boots and bad attitudes they had at the bar. They were roommates, and people were always trying to figure out if they were girlfriends. No one knew anyone either of them had slept with, but they weren't very affectionate with each other either.

　　　　　　　　　　　　　　　ROBIN SWEENEY

Sam suspected they both sublimated their sex drives into their pool games. They played very, very good pool.

They were doing that bar conversation where everyone is talking and no one is quite listening. Then Larry spoke, loudly enough to shut the three of them up.

"Hey, Jo. You doing it with other boys now? Turning into a faggot, huh?"

Shit, Sam swore to herself. For a couple of girls who looked like rejects from a remake of *Cruising* they sure were being cruel to other butches. She hoped they didn't freak Jo out and scare the boy off. She hated the shit she got from other butches about being into butch women more than the flak she sometimes got from femmes. At least femmes understood butch attraction, even if it made them a little pissy when butches went off together. A butch who wasn't into butches could dish some really weird and twisted homophobic stuff.

Jo was blushing as she shook her head no. "Sam's just my brother."

Mike and Larry seemed to like that and, with arm-punching good-byes, left them to play more pool.

Sam turned to Jo and gave her a long hard look. At least the boy had the good grace to look away.

"Just your brother? Well, now. You gonna give your big brother a ride home on your bike and see what happens, even if I'm just your brother?"

Sam got Jo by the collar of her jacket almost before she turned her bike off. She pulled Jo's arm up behind her back and marched her up the stairs to the front door. She managed to get the door open with Jo squirming and complaining and shoved the boy in and up against the wall. Held her by her throat, just to get her attention.

"Listen to me, boy. This isn't a game, and this isn't about being an asshole. I know what kind of a boy you can be, and I want you to be that good, boy."

Sam opened Jo's leather jacket and pulled her tank top out of her pants and up above her tits, grabbing her nipple. With the other hand, she opened her own jacket and vest and let Jo get at her tits. Jo responded like a dream to Sam's twisting and tugging and tried not to cry out when Sam got her nipple between her fingernails. Sam worked both the boy's nipples into hard, brown rocks and started slapping and punching her chest.

"Yeah, you fucking stud you. You work out at the gym every day, getting this body together and hard so that someone can come along and hurt you. And nobody hurts you enough. Nobody hits you hard enough, or pushes you far enough. You're good and all that, but being a good boy isn't all you want, right? You want to be able to wrestle and push and fight back and still be taken down, right? You want to have to be good because you want to be good and somebody meaner than you made you do it, huh?"

Jo started moaning a little bit as Sam pummeled her. She punched Jo's chest and arms, put her knee between her legs and shoved it against her crotch. Jo was talking back at her now, saying yes, saying no, saying she didn't know who would win this, saying please. Sam had guessed right about some of Jo's buttons, and the boy was very turned on. Jo had started working Sam's tit-rings, and was pulling them almost as hard as Sam was punching her.

"That's right, you get to fight back. I take it as long as you take what I give you. Until I decide it's enough."

At that, Sam slapped Jo's face hard, right and left and then right again. Jo put her hands back against the wall (which was just as well. Sam's tits hadn't been healed long, and it was starting to really hurt. It doesn't do to yelp the first time you're taking a boy down).

"You're ready to do this?" Sam asked, her nose an inch away from Jo's, both of them breathing hard.

Jo nodded.

"I can't hear you," Sam said.

"Yeah."

"What?"

"Yes, I'm ready?"

"Wrong." Sam slapped Jo again, whose dark eyes were beginning to looked confused and mad in addition to horny. "You call me 'Sir' when we do this, boy. Try again."

"Yes, Sir, I'm ready, Sir?"

"That's better."

Sam shoved Jo down the hall and into her room. She had unfolded her futon before she left for the bar and had put her toys within reach. It wasn't an extensive collection, but Sam was pretty pleased with the range of sensations she could create. She grabbed Jo and kissed her hard. Sam had wanted to get this boy in her room for so long she broke her own rule about kissing on the first date. It was all right to beat somebody, or get hurt herself, but kissing was different. Kissing was intimate and close.

No matter. Jo's mouth tasted like cigarettes and something minty and sex. Sam leaned into the kiss, searching and finding answers to questions that frightened her. Sam was nearly breathless when she finally pulled herself away and shoved Jo to her knees.

Sam had taken a risk and bought a new piece of chain for Jo's collar. She pulled it out of her pocket and put it around Jo's neck, locking it into place and pulling Jo's head back to look into her eyes.

"There anything you want to say?"

Jo looked at Sam and then took a deep breath.

"Sir, I've never done this before." At Sam's bark of laughter, the boy got defensive. "I've never done it with someone I called 'Sir,' before. Sir. You know, another boy. I've only bottomed for femme tops before. Sir."

Sam looked at Jo and stepped back. She kept eye contact with Jo and stripped off her jacket, tossing it in the corner. Sam then ran her hand down over her belt buckle and the bulge in her pants. She ran her fingers down her cock until Jo got the idea and dropped her eyes to crotch level. When Sam had first wandered into a sex shop, finally deciding to make her fantasies into realities, she found a copy of the *Leatherman's Handbook*. Larry Townsend's diatribe about how a bottom had to know how to suck dick made an impression on Sam that started her on the road to being a very different kind of dyke.

"Well," Sam said, "some things are a little different. Your mistress ever teach you how to put a rubber on with your teeth?"

The boy had gotten the hang of it, eventually, and learned the difference between being called a cocksucker in a friendly way and having your face fucked to learn who was in charge. Jo seemed surprised Sam could actually come from having her plastic sex-toy attachment sucked, and Sam made a mental note to teach this boy a little bit about packing a dick.

Sam sent the boy down on the ground to work on her boots and give her a chance to tuck her cock back in her pants. Then she reached down, grabbed Jo by the belt and tossed her onto her futon. Jo growled at shifting gears from sweet boot-chewing to being treated like a sack of potatoes. Sam fell on top of her, and they wrestled.

Once the wrestling was done, Jo had lost her boots and her pants — Sam was glad to see that Jo was the kind of boy who didn't wear underwear — and gained a pair of wrist restraints that tied her spread-eagled and face up on Sam's futon. Sam had a series of bite marks from her neck to her chest. They had wrestled seriously for a while, tossing each other against the bed and the wall, with Jo's height advantage giving her an edge.

At one point, Jo had Sam face down with her knee in her back.

"Ask me," Sam managed to choke out, trying to grab at Jo and failing.

"Huh? Ask you what?"

That break in concentration was what Sam had needed, and she pushed Jo up and off her back and got her by the chain around her neck.

"Ask me permission to laugh, boy." Sam then tickled her until she begged Sam to stop. Part of being a top, Sam had found, was taking advantage of whatever dirty tricks became available.

The rest of the scene had been exploration, seeing what Sam had that Jo did and didn't like and what she would and wouldn't take. It was hardly safe, sane and consensual, but that night was possibly the hottest sex Sam had ever had. They hadn't done negotiations with each of them having a list of dos and don'ts and what-ifs. Instead, Sam would push, and Jo would either give in or try to get away, and it didn't seem to bother either of them. The times Jo said "no," Sam was able to figure out it really meant no and stopped. The boy had courage.

Jo didn't care for the needles that Sam had put through her upper arm, although she toughed it out until Sam had pulled them out. The boy was a pig, though, when Sam covered her chest and stomach with clothespins and played with them until Jo laughed and then yowled. She only tried to get away when Sam started removing them with her riding crop.

Sam had guessed right; Jo liked to be hit hard. The boy liked the drumsticks that Sam worked her thighs with, leaving deep bruises that would continue to rise for another three days. Sam turned her over and flogged her back for what seemed liked hours, until Jo broke down and cried and then asked for more. (At that point, Sam was pretty certain she was in love with this boy, even if only for one night.) Jo hated the cane that Sam brought down across her ass — convincing Sam to be a little less in love but still smitten — but put up with it enough to call Sam an asshole.

But when Sam started taking off her belt to administer a few discipline blows for bad language, Jo gave her a real "no," up on her knees and pulling Sam's futon with her, trying to get away from what was obviously not Sam but someone else, older and meaner and ages ago. Sam dropped her belt and landed on Jo with her full weight. Trying to keep someone grounded while they fought with an old demon and cried for the second time in a night was part of what came with the territory, although it scared Sam almost as much as it scared Jo.

Then when the boy had stopped crying and finally relaxed, not noticing that Sam had taken the restraints off and her dick out, the fucking started. Slow at first, playing with the boy's ass and trying to open it up, feeding the boy's ass with lube, both of them growling and moaning and trying to see if it would work. Then faster and crazy and howling until Jo gave it up, hollering and coming under Sam and begging her not to let it stop. Sam put Jo on her back and then put her gloved hand into her, fucking Jo with a fury she didn't recognize until Sam swore she would never be able to move her arm again.

THEY SLEPT hard after the sex that first night, Sam barely able to stay awake long enough to make Jo pull her boots and lube-covered gloves and dick off. Sam kept Jo's collar on, and Jo didn't ask for it to be taken off. Sam tucked Jo's butt against her belly and held onto her until they both fell asleep. Jo woke up early in the morning before it was light, and chewed on Sam's neck enough for her to roll over. Jo figured out pretty quickly how to pin Sam down and give her back what she wanted.

It had been pretty much like that since then, although it was hard to get Jo to commit to a date past next week. They'd had some adventures since then. At the new women's sex club, they'd picked up a very cute femme from Amsterdam who told them in three different languages that she loved their fists. Since that night, the two of them had taken up monthly residence at one of the club's slings, taking on any of the girls who wanted a couple of butches. It was an interesting sort of male bonding. They never fucked each other at the club, but would go home and stay up far into the morning working off the pent-up hunger.

For her birthday, Jo had met Sam up in Collingwood Park, and they had attracted a crowd of cheering faggots while they fucked in the bushes. Jo had leaned against a tree and made Sam suck her off, and then fucked her from behind. (Jo had learned quickly about having a handle on her dick.) The boys loved it. Later that night, at Sam's house, Jo gave her a copy of her bike key, in case Sam ever needed to borrow it. Sam took it as a sign of some sort of commitment. But later, in a vulnerable moment after sex and ice cream, when Sam told Jo it was the best birthday a girlfriend had ever done for her, Jo exploded. She started yelling about how she didn't like being pressured and couldn't they just be buddies? The two of them had a horrible fight, and Sam had stormed off, furious that her birthday had been screwed up and terrified that this fight was the beginning of the end. They had been careful with each other since then, afraid to talk about this already-fragile matter.

Sam wanted a girlfriend she knew was her girlfriend. Was that totally impossible with another butch, or just this particular butch?

Jo came into the kitchen, dressed for her shift at the café. "You OK, bud?" she asked, trying to get Sam's attention. She knew Sam's best moments were not in the morning, but usually she didn't hang out, lost in space and naked in front of the coffee pot.

"Oh, yeah. Just a little worn out from last night, you animal." Sam smiled at her as Jo swallowed her coffee and leaned over the table to kiss her.

"I'm off at seven. Come by and pick me up, if you want. We can do dinner or something," Jo said, as she put her jacket on and headed out the door.

Yeah, right, of course, Sam thought as the door closed. *It's always going to be easy and weird and not quite solid. Just significant buddies. Shit.* Sam put the coffee mugs in the sink and went back down the hall to her room. She'd go back to sleep or jack off to make herself feel better. She refused to cry over that stupid boy and this stupid relationship and bit her lip to keep the tears from starting.

Jo had made the bed and piled everything else in one corner of her room. There was a gym bag in the middle of her futon. Jo had written a note and taped it to the bag.

"I hope you don't mind, but I'll be back tonight, and I thought I should keep this stuff here."

Nestled in several pairs of Jo's underwear and socks were her dick and harness. Sam laughed at how significant a sex toy could be. Feeling cheerier, she decided to go out to breakfast at the café where Jo worked. Maybe she could get a deal since she was boffing the cook.

Dyke Daddies

Linnea Due

HANDS fidget, eyes roll, legs are crossed and recrossed. Finally the dam bursts. "Daddy, can't I be excused, *please?*" It's an entreaty heard in millions of households across the nation — except this time the speaker is a twenty-seven-year-old woman — and "Daddy," three years older, is an annual participant in Gay Freedom Day's Dykes on Bikes contingent.

This scene wouldn't go over big in Peoria — but does it even pass muster in the women's leather community? When I brought up the subject of dyke daddies to some S/M pals, the remarks were not encouraging.

"Who would want to play with incest?" asked one woman.

"It reminds me of the fall of Rome," said another.

"You *can* go too far, you know," reminded a third.

And yet, when the First Annual Dyke Daddy Contest was held in San Francisco in 1992, it attracted a full house of spectators and participants as well as a panel of judges who chose B.C. Cliver as the winner.

"I don't think dyke daddies are a fad," Cliver says. "I think of it more as another facet of women's sexuality that's finally come to the surface. The feelings were always there, only now there's a label for them. 'Daddy' is a lot closer to who I am than 'Mistress.'"

No argument there. Cliver, thirty, who freelances as a personal trainer at a number of gyms in San Francisco, is a bodybuilder and looks it. She flexes her biceps, tips her black leather cap forward, and waves a finger at her "little girl," twenty-seven-year-old Bobbi Marshall. Marshall snaps to, fetching a spoon so Cliver can muddle the foam in her cappuccino.

"Part of it's being a butch top," Cliver continues, after she thanks Marshall with a grin. "But being a daddy means there's a lot of tenderness involved. Maybe it allows butch dykes to give the kind of nurturing you can as a mother. After all, most of us aren't going to have children."

We don't usually associate topping with nurturing — yet anyone who enjoys playing with power knows there's a lot of nurturing on both sides of the S/M equation. And that emphasis on caring — the protective cloak that daddy wraps around his charges — is, according to everyone I talked to, the single most unifying characteristic of daddy play.

Why then are my buddies sounding the death knell of Western civilization?

A participant at a recent seminar on daddy play had a partial answer: "I hesitated to attend this program," she admitted. "It's too intimate. And it's really different for each person. Some people have been incested and are really into playing daddy. It helps them deal with their childhood experiences. And some haven't and are into it. And some people are just really upset about it, both those who've survived incest and those who didn't have to deal with that."

"When I'm being daddy," she continued, " — and I don't feel like I'm *playing* — the person I am with one lover isn't the same person I am with someone else. And however daunting a role may appear — like if I'm supposed to be an abuser — when I'm in that role I'm in a delicate and vulnerable place."

This observation struck a nerve, because a number of tops leapt in to complain that bottoms assume they're all-powerful.

"They think you're their parents, and they start unleashing all this hostility on you," one woman said.

Another woman agreed. "I know. I never thought when I got into this that I could end up with a rebellious teenager on my hands. When you take on this dynamic, it's fraught. Age play, incest, those kinds of taboos can be really scary. But playing daddy doesn't have to be about incest at all."

B.C. Cliver agrees. In fact, when I mention incest to her, she grimaces. "I know too many women who've been incested for that to appeal to me. I've done a couple incest scenes and it was hot, but afterwards both the bottom and I were really unsettled. I understand how other people could enjoy it, but it's not for me."

Cliver's "little girl" is nodding. "Even without incest," says Marshall, "some stuff about playing daddy is hard. My father was an alcoholic with a volcanic temper. He used to order us around — get me this, do that. Then along comes B.C. At first when she'd tell me to get her something, I'd cringe. We had to work it out. I can answer back with her. When she gets short-tempered, most of the time she's hungry. I tell her to go eat a bagel. I could never do that with my father. He might kill me."

Cliver says she started playing daddy when she was in a relationship with a woman who had a dog. "Whenever I walked in the door, the dog would start jumping around, and my girlfriend would say, 'Daddy's home.' It just fell into line." She touches Marshall's hand. "When I met this one, I told her that's how I wanted it to be."

Marshall, a strawberry blonde who's a peer counselor and student at San Francisco City College, smiles. "When B.C. said she wanted to be my daddy, she told me to pick an age. 'What are you talking about?' I said. 'I've got an age!'"

Cliver shakes her head. "Obnoxious," she tells me.

Marshall continues without a hitch. "Then she told me about these couples where the kids were like seven or eight. We both looked at each other and said, 'No way.'" They both laugh. "So the most we've managed is like, sixteen. Oh, sometimes I'll go littler, if I want something, or if I'm being punished. But what I really am is a rebellious teenager."

It seems one daddy's nightmare is another daddy's wet dream. Cliver and Marshall couldn't be more tickled with each other — they're constantly stroking, touching, smiling. Marshall informs me that her straight friends accept Cliver as her daddy.

"They have to," she says with a defiant adolescent shrug. "That's the way it is."

Cliver says S/M enters the picture as both punishment and reward. "If I really need to punish her, I'll do it with something that's borderline nonconsensual."

"Oh, don't use that word," Marshall objects. "I agreed to all this."

"I just mean I use an implement she doesn't like. In her case it's a Fiberglas cane."

Marshall sneaks me a wink. Daddy clearly doesn't know everything.

"The thing that pisses me off," said one daddy at the seminar, "are these kids who come over to play with my kids and expect me to be their dad, too. I think that's really inappropriate."

"Of course it is!" a woman cried into the din of general agreement. "It's sexual, for god's sakes."

And therein, for many, lies the rub. Sex and kids don't go together, even if the "kids" are on the wrong side of forty. It's an interesting exercise in how fantasy, roles, and reality can slide around, merging in ways we might not expect. I discovered, for instance, that the assumed age of the kid made a difference to me. Under fifteen started straying into the realm of what I considered nonconsensual, in that the power imbalance is too great for the child to give authentic and meaningful consent. I had to keep reminding myself that everyone was over twenty-one. And I wasn't the only one slipping and sliding.

"My first scene was around incest," one seminar participant said. "The woman I was playing with had chosen to be around six or seven, and the idea was that I, as daddy, went from being a good person to being an abuser. I found that I had to move out of role to fuck her. I had my own incest experiences to deal with. I felt like things were breaking up inside of me, part of me was dying. I just couldn't take on that role."

For some people, though, rewriting painful history is what this is all about. "I've had girlfriends who haven't known they were incest survivors until they discovered it with me," one woman said. "We've had to be OK with the fact that it's hot. I think you have to rip the scab off and let it bleed before it can be healed."

"Look," another woman said, "the big difference is that the bottom's turned on. I'm a top who's willing to deal with someone else's nightmare. Tops take on these stigmatized identities so other people can work through their shit. But it's how S/M operates; it's always paradoxical. You hurt to give someone pleasure; you tie someone up to give them a liberating experience."

"You take on a great responsibility when you play with these loaded topics," one woman cautioned. "You're probably going to be dealing with abandonment issues. Shit can and will come up, but the likelihood is that you're going to get back as much as you give."

"Part of my agenda was to be a better dad than my own dad,"

another woman noted. "But after dealing with bottoms, I started to realize why he was such an asshole."

"The kids have such a marvelous freedom from responsibility," one woman agreed. "They're always obnoxious, always testing."

OK, we get it that daddies are vulnerable — but how about the kids? Those attending the seminar had evidently been told that children should be seen and not heard, so I set up an appointment with Ann Wertheim, who's written a number of short stories and articles on the daddy theme.

Wertheim, thirty, has short hair and a mobile face that's exceptionally soft and open. She's manager of the Gauntlet in San Francisco, a one-stop piercing emporium where they perform the piercing and sell you the jewelry to adorn it. Wertheim herself has a tongue piercing, but it's only visible in rare flashes. She leans towards me and divulges that she's had punishment fantasies since she was four or five.

"At first they weren't sexual," she says. "Well no, that's wrong. At first they weren't *genital.* They were always sexual. They were fantasies of being spanked or chastised by someone older, like a camp counselor or a teacher. When I met this woman who was turned on by daddy stories in *Drummer* magazine, it just clicked." She pauses. "She was significantly older, fifteen years' difference. When we broke up, she said it was too much responsibility. I think what really happened is that *she* felt too responsible. I may be a little girl, but I'm an adult, too."

The odd part of this is that while both Marshall and Wertheim *are* adult, not to mention thoughtful and articulate, there's a part of them that corresponds to the age they've chosen. Wertheim is almost kittenish as she sips at her Calistoga and explains how she found her alter ego.

"At first I didn't have an age for my little girl. Then things began evolving. Once an incest component came in, I got an age, around ten to twelve. See, I've always told myself stories, but lately I've been able to verbalize them. Now my girlfriend adds sexy elements. It's like she can get inside my head and tell my story."

She glances up to see if I understand. "What's happening with our story now is that I've never had sex with anyone except my daddy. Just recently daddy decided to bring mommy into this. daddy doesn't want to fuck mommy anymore. He just wants to fuck his little girl and mommy has to stand around and watch."

"Is mommy real?" I ask.

Wertheim shakes her head. "No. Though once I did play with a mommy. She was maternal, a big nurturing woman. Now that everyone else in the world is into daddy, I should move on to mommy." She laughs. "Except it wouldn't work. I like butch women too much."

Where exactly does butch leave off and daddy begin? For that matter, how do top and daddy differ? Jacquie Hansen explains that dad is responsible for his charge's welfare in a way that butches and tops are not. Above all, being daddy means being protective.

At thirty-nine, Hansen has short hair and a braided tail. She parks her motorcycle on the sidewalk in front of the café and shrugs off her jacket. Moments later, her kid arrives, a "little boy" who says she wants to remain incognito. "My business could suffer," she explains.

Hansen sends her off to get water. I'm beginning to see the advantages of playing daddy — these adult kids are much more serviceable than the usual kind.

Hansen seems surprised when I ask about incest. "Well," she says, "that element is always there underneath. Whether you've been incested or not, anger and hurt feelings can come up. But I'm not the person who caused those feelings. I'm a loving, caring daddy. I'm in control of who daddy is."

The boy comes back with the water and asks permission to tell me that while Daddy may be strict, he is never abusive.

"Our parents weren't listening to us," Hansen affirms as she pats the couch next to her and her boy obediently sits. "If there's a problem with one of my little boys or girls, we can talk about it." Whenever Hansen makes a point by thrusting her hand in the air, her boy catches the hand on the downswing, capturing daddy's hand in her lap until the next emphatic gesture.

Hansen began playing daddy when she was living in Greece. "The people I was living with started referring to me as their daddy. They saw me as the kind of father they wanted to have."

"Were these people adult women?"

Hansen nods.

"Did this daddy play include S/M?"

"I don't just do S/M in scene," Hansen explains. "I live S/M. I'm a multitude of things, and being daddy is part of it."

Is being a daddy something that arises in context or is it a gut knowledge about yourself? Did women know, the way they might have known they were butch, that they were daddies when they were, say, ten?

"It's part of me, sure," says Cliver, "but it's brought out by another person. Let's say it's *awakened* by someone else."

Hansen has "always been stern and to the point, and people identified that as being parental." She shrugs. "I'm a leader. I tend to carry people with me. People feel they can be vulnerable around me. But as a top I'm vulnerable, too. Both the daddy top and the top top can be soft and stern, but it's another kind of soft and stern. It's just a different persona."

Ann Wertheim says she knew her destiny from an early age. "The daddy stuff is my heart," she says. "It's more at my core than being a lesbian. Sometimes I feel alienated from the S/M community — whips and chains and handcuffs don't resonate for me because they aren't what parents would use on their kids. Top/bottom involves my intellect and my body, but not my spirit."

What is it that daddy brings to dykes? The fact that daddies have always been popular in the gay male community is no surprise: Men don't have a lot of roles that allow tenderness, and daddy/boy is a perfect script for the nurturing men crave but are rarely allowed. But aren't dykes light years beyond that stifled state of affairs? Aren't two women the very embodiment of empathy and caring? Sounds suspiciously like what your straight friends say when they've decided they want to sample the wares on the other side of the sexual-orientation fence.

"I guess daddies like it because they get all this trust," Wertheim says, shoulders moving, head moving, as if she can't stand to be demure in this café a second longer; she just has to break out in loud purrs. "I really am a little kid inside. The very best thing about daddy is that he loves you no matter what."

What about mommy? Isn't this stuff kind of antifeminist?

"Daddy's an archetype," says Jacquie Hansen. "I think lesbians have become willing to be more vulnerable, to let things in that are scary."

And, of course, the daddy a dyke becomes, no matter how reflective of her experiences with men or with her own father, is still a female creation. Said one woman at the seminar, "When I'm playing daddy, I'm professorial, wearing wing-tips, smoking a pipe, just like my father. He was an ice-cold man. Now I get to know who he would have been if he had laughed."

So it's not the collapse of Rome, nor is it even particularly startling, though for many people there's an inherent problem with using age play to establish roles in a relationship. In a top/bottom dynamic, even one that's played out twenty-four hours a day, both parties function as adults, and both can take care of the other within the confines of their roles. The same is true of butch/femme. But with daddy/kid, one is being a parent and one a child. In order to interact and communicate as adults, both have to step out of their roles, and given that the roles are sexualized, this can create a layer of confusion just where you don't want it.

Feeling that one must always be a parent is, I suspect, what's behind the complaint that being a daddy is "too much responsibility." Yet, if the individuals involved have the right psychological "wiring" to find daddy play not only a turn-on but deeply fulfilling, then they have the motivation to overcome that difficulty.

Although some women live daddy/kid full time, probably many more choose an element of age play that appeals to them and is psychically less threatening — an unrelated older friend, say, or a flirtation with the baby-sitter — and inject it as spice into their sex lives on an occasional basis. Even a brief dabble with these kinds of characters can be challenging — and not only to those who have been incested. After all, we're social animals; civilization requires that we accept certain rules to be accepted into the "tribe" — whether our family or the community. For some women, eroticizing those ancient truths in a setting where both partners have control can be freeing and inspiring.

"I think of my daddy as a bear rug who can cover me no matter how strong I am," says one woman. And, as Jacquie Hansen says, "It's good that people are able to be daddies, because there's a lot of little boys and girls out there who need us."

Confessions of a Dyke Daddy

JACKIE WELTMAN

I WAS a daddy exiled. Exiled from Oneonta in the autumn. Right about the time the community was smack-dab into its succession of holiday potlucks, I chose to pack up and go rather than endure their judgment. A maverick. A lonely, tough soul going it alone. But — hey — that's the kind of guy I am. As I threw my bowling shirts into my suitcase, Zonker telephoned.

"Yo."

"Pops — this is Zonk. They're having a cosmetics burning ceremony tonight."

"A what?"

"They're planning to burn cosmetics — because of what you did to Licorice. They've consensed on a buying agent and a bonfire committee. The buying agent went and bought out the Maybelline display at K-Mart. The committee is going to Moss Woods tonight to burn it at the spot where you and Licorice had your little... thing. You know, to kind of like — exorcise — the, uh, negative karma... of the spot."

Burn cosmetics? Burnt flakes of waterproof mascara all over the environment?

What a dumb-ass idea.

THIS ALL started with Licorice, fickle little androgyne temptress. She had a figure, whoa — chestnuts. None too many visible figures in Oneonta. But like my grandpop always said, "*il giardino é morte, comunque devî mangiare*," which, loosely translated from the Italian, means "the garden is wilted — you still gotta eat." Seems every babe in Oneonta was destroyed at the flush, taut beginning of her babeness. She'd arrive a young, raw-but-educated junior feminist with ... *tendencies*, shall we say; a graceful application of eye shadow on her lids, a slash of cinnamon pink lipstick on the near-virgin lips, ready for action. *Right?*

No. The Radical University Womyn's Clob (not club ... clubs are for boys) would jump her heart the minute she hit the Oneonta State University campus. Smothered in a cult-style brainwash of tofu and Andrea Dworkin, our hapless, ripe little babe loses her juicy glow. She is bereft of hair, pumped with theory, and dressed in a tee-shirt from the 1978 Michigan Womyn's Music Festival. With the nose of papa wolf, I sense potential. Then it is gone.

So it was with Licorice. She had potential in the firm little nipples department. I met her at the September potluck of Lavender Bowling Womyn. I wore my nattiest red and gray Pin-Tigers bowling shirt.

"I'm Poppy, but you can call me Pops," I shook her hand.

"I used to be Angela, but now I'm Licorice," she purred, her purple "Take Back the Night" tee-shirt a little bit tighter than all the other girls'.

AFTER SEVERAL bowling dates, I figured she still liked me, so I asked her for a romantic walk in Moss Woods. I had the spot picked out and some stuff waiting for us there: blankets, latex, lingerie, beers, manacles, a blowtorch, cosmetics. I figured she'd like it. I mean — hey.

I spread out the blankets; we started making out hotly. I offered her a beer, but she said she didn't drink. Then, naturally, I wanted to know: Was she going to be my little girl for the night?

"Your what?"

"My little girlie baby, my baby woman girlsky, my babesky adolescent womanchild ..."

She screwed up her nose for a minute, then tried to be tender with me. Tender, I like that.

"Poppy, I'm a womon — not a girl. I've spent years of my life ... womyn spent years of their lives fighting for me to be a womon. I didn't know you were into S/M. Poppy, I'm sorry — I think it's male behavior."

"Who's talking S/M, honey-pie? I just want to see you in this."

I flourished the peach-mauve teddy. She softened. It was my charm, and we got the shirt off. Her nipples were peach-mauve. Zonga. Yow.

But for some reason the karma of that night was not grooving entirely with me. "How old are you tonight, sweetie? Old enough for makeup?" I was getting ready to pull out my dildo and rub it against her fluffy natural cunt.

"Excuse me?" She leveled her eyes at me. They swerved intensively from side to side like a late-model corvette in a GM performance test commercial.

"Are you fifteen, baby, sixteen? Old enough for working papers? Like, let's put some lipstick on." I pulled out the cosmetics bag from under a pile of leaves. "You're a big girl now, right? Old enough to put on lipstick and leave it all over daddy's dick . . ."

"Daddy!?"

"Yeah, beautiful, what's the problem?"

"You never told me you were into being . . . *daddy*."

"You've been calling me Poppy all this time."

"I thought you meant the *flower*!" she groaned, and, as her jaw dropped, ripped off the pretty teddy and backed away with her hastily gathered clothing like a breastplate in front of her. Then she ran, her pert nipples forever a memory.

I pulled out my blowtorch and lit up a pile of sticks. "Well, fuck it all!" I hollered, and it echoed off the roof of the Lavender Sisterhood Coffeehouse. I had another beer, lit up a cigar, and roasted the teddy.

NEXT DAY — that's when Zonker called me. Zonk is my buddy. She is, like, my spy. She lives here, of all places, because she's got a good job. She goes to all the lesbian events. Everybody respects her. She tells them she's being celibate right now — getting her head together. She lets me know all the dirt kicked up behind my back. She sympathizes with me.

Because Zonk is a guy. A Puerto Rican guy. She used to be Xavier. Then she started taking hormones, got electrolysis and changed it to something gender-neutral.

"The Estrada St. Womyn's Potluck Brunch Committee is calling for a womyncott of you," she warned. "Poppy, your name is ash, junk. Don't try to get in anywhere on a sliding scale in this town anymore. No more concerts — you've been eighty-sixed from the Lavender Womyn's Potluck Brunch Supper Club. They've even alerted the ASPCA. Forget about adopting that cat."

"Isn't that a little extreme?"

"Well, the reasoning goes — like, you might try to do something to, or *with*, the cat."

I wanted some chick to wear makeup and suck my dildo and they think I want to fuck a cat.

"Zonk, they want me out, I'm out. Basta. In fact, as we speak, I am throwing my favorite bowling shirts into my suitcase. Go Greyhound. You can have my Frank Sinatra records."

"Wow. Really?"

"And I'll throw in *Dean Martin Sings Live at Radio City* because I love ya', diamond butt."

Zonk was silent for a while. My heart ached. Then she spoke.

"Pops, I'm coming with you."

"Ah, fungool; you're full of it."

"No, really, I've been thinking about this for a while. I'm living a lie here. Is being the Chief Loan Officer of the Lavender Womyn's Incorporated Credit Union worth the *agony* of lying to everyone I know every day? Do you know the last time I saw another Puerto Rican dyke in this town? Eh? 1978! Not to mention another lesbian transsexual! I'm sick of it Popster," her voice was rising, "and now all of this shit with you. *I* have a car, and we'd both get out of here a lot faster together."

Zonk wasn't kidding: she had a restored 1968 Olds with a dark red body and cream-colored fins. Lines as smooth as a cheerleader's breasts.

On our way out of town, we could see the smoke rising from south Moss Woods.

AFTER ALMOST four hundred miles and eight hours, heading down to I-80, we found ourselves in Meadville, PA. We were ready to have some drinks and find a place to pass out. We cruised the strip. Quincy's Bohemian Lounge looked ripe. There was a curvaceous brunette thing in the corner booth. Looked about fifteen. Upon closer inspection, I noticed her psycho biker tattoos, knife holster, and her fringed black miniskirt. I do believe she'd made it out of drapes. I looked around. No biker dudes in sight. Zonga. Wah.

Zonk went belly up to the bar, and after I ordered my Ovaltine, I struck up a conversation with her about traveling, living life on the road, the wind-in-your-hair kind of freedom that could only be experienced by one on the wild highways of this wide America — and although I didn't have any hair; well, fuck it. You know, how "hair" is, like, in your "mind" — and, naturally, the conversation progressed along the "hair" line until we got to the subject of pubes. What color were hers? How thick? Had she had them long? Did she have, like, any exciting physical reaction when she imagined shaving them off? She was digging it, and my hand was finding its way up her pubescent thigh when, out of the corner of my eye, I noticed large shapes... they were... sweatshirts — two large sweatshirts — menacingly approaching Zonk at the bar. I squinted closely at them. Big yellow letters: "Theta... Beta... Xi." Shit. Sherri's (her name was Sherri) delicate blond thigh hairs were stirring under my fingers...and Zonk was throwing terrified, alarmed looks at me. I excused myself.

"Ah-hah, here's another one, Brian."

Sloshed frat vermin. What would Frank Sinatra do?

"Dykes, man. Get the hell out of here."

"I'm not feelin' real good right now," I replied, "Could you leave us alone?"

"I'm sooo sorry." Brian, the taller one, pugnaciously stepped closer. "C'mon Hal." His hair was buzzed unevenly in a pathetic attempt to be hip.

"Not now, fellas."

"That's right — I'm a fella, dyke. My dick's bigger than yours... and it squirts!"*

"Not now, man. Daddy has her period."

They cracked up.

You know what I hate the most? I hate it when people don't take me seriously.

* *Author's Note: Somebody actually once said this to me!*

JACKIE WELTMAN

"I SAID Daddy has her PERiod. GodDAMNit." Pow! Thunk. "Don't fuck with Daddy … when we have our PERiod." Pow! Thunk.

Chaos. Four of us were tumbling all over the floor with our mouths full of sawdust. The bartender was gingerly dialing the phone. Suddenly, a shrill "Fuck OFF SLIME pit!" It was Sherri — black pump in one hand, hunting knife in the other. *Baby.*

The frat slime actually did shrink back. "Goddamn cunts," spluffed a black and blue Hal from a low corner.

Zonk sprang up. She unzipped her trousers ever so delicately. She has a cute little dick, if a bit shriveled. It bobbled to and fro, almost in time to Garth Brooks crooning from the jukebox.

"Hal — you have a cute little butt there," I offered.

They were speechless. Freaked. Silence. Smiles. Ha.

It took about ten seconds for the three of us to tear out and screech to the first stop light. Sherri delicately folded her hunting knife back into its leather holster.

We drove to a motel with Sherri. I found out in between make-out sessions that she was a teenage runaway staying with her closet-case biology teacher "for now." We urged her to come with us — what had she got to lose? We'd decided to go to California where we could be at home among freaks. We drank tequila, whooped and partied all that night to Meadville radio. This exile thing was not so bad.

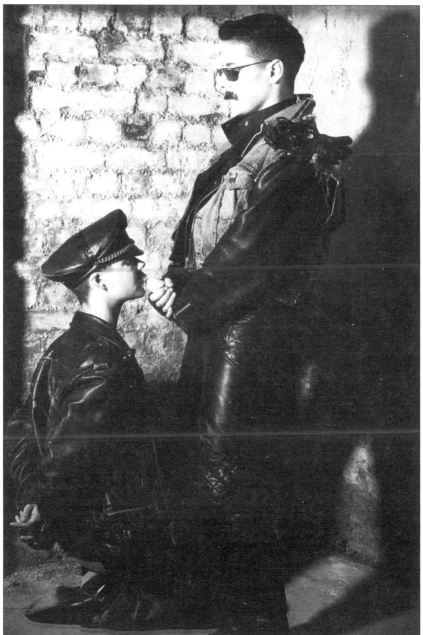

DELLA GRACE

Combat Boots and Helium Heels

An Interview with Tribe 8's Lynn Breedlove

LILY BURANA

LYNN *Breedlove, thirty-four, is the lead singer/lyricist for Tribe 8, a San Francisco-based punk-dyke band. With provocative songs such as "Frat Pig" (which petitions that the proper retribution for drunken frat boys who gang rape is a turnabout round of gang castration) and "Lesbophobia" (an anthemic taunting of lesbophobic straight girls), the band has garnered an enthusiastic following of rowdy, radical women and men alike, from the Pacific Northwest to Northern Europe.*

There are several things that distinguish a Tribe 8 performance from your average punk rock show. First off is the occasional presence of a mostly-female slam dance pit. Second is Breedlove herself. She is arguably the most visible, if not the only, butch front-woman in punk today, a status she flaunts with equal measures of gusto, grace, and humor. Within the first few songs of a set, she almost always doffs her shirt and roams the stage clad only in a pair of baggy jeans and boots. Then, she often whips a gargantuan dildo out of her pants, merging the concepts of crowd-control and mind-fuck as jaws drop, minds tweak, and more often than you'd think, boys, both straight and queer, come forward to worship the rubber behemoth.

Breedlove generously invited me to her apartment in San Francisco's Outer Mission to share her philosophy about butchness, bottoming, and exposing her breasts.

Lily Burana: So tell me, why do you take off your shirt on stage?
Lynn Breedlove: For one thing, it's hot up there! What do dudes

do in that situation? They take off their shirt! And I got nice tits; why shouldn't I be able to show them off?

There's a whole political aspect to going topless, too. I refuse to let men decide when I can show my tits, or when they're gonna make money off of me showing my tits. That's a whole exploitative deal that I just don't feel like being a part of. So taking my shirt off on stage is a three-pronged statement: Number one, I'm just more comfortable that way; number two, I'm proud of my tits and I want people to look at them; and number three, FUCK YOU!

Lily: Do guys in the audience ever misconstrue it as a sexual thing?

Lynn: Yeah. But for men to view it as a statement of sexual availability, they have to be either really stupid or trying to fuck with me because my attitude on stage is just like, "I know you're here to look at my tits, so quit looking at my tits, MOTHERFUCKER! I'm not here for your amusement. My shirt's off cuz I'm hot, not so you can drool all over me!" My attitude is really out there and aggressive. It's not all sexy and come fuck me. I'm practically standing there with a knife wielded at their fly so if they don't get it ...

This one guy from Wichita, Kansas did send a letter, saying "Oh, you really turn me on, you just haven't had the right man," and the whole fucking deal. At first I was like, what the fuck? And then I realized that he was just trying to fuck with me, but I couldn't tell if that's because he was stupid, crazy or totally threatened, and this was the only way he knew how to get back at me.

Lily: What about women in the audience?

Lynn: Women can really get into it! At that particular show in Wichita, two chicks took their shirts off, then they made their other pal take her shirt off, and they're standing there half naked with their shirts off, then there was this other girl wedged into the corner trying to hide, and these girls started chanting her name and stuff until she finally took her shirt off, too. Then we had five totally gorgeous babes dancing around in the front row with their shirts off. It was hotter than fuck in there, too. It was great!

Lily: Do you ever attract girl groupies?

Lynn: Yeah, I guess that's happened on occasion. Once in England, Kat, our old drummer, she totally started snoggin' her face off with this chick, and they had a little hot affair after the show. So I guess it was a star-fucking thing, I don't know.

Girls have written us letters saying that they have a crush on me or on Flipper [one of the guitarists in the band, butchy in appearance], but the actual physical manifestation rarely happens. I never notice, though, when anyone has the hots for me. You have to hit me over the head with a two-by-four. I'm just oblivious. "Why would you like me, duh?"

Lily: Does your girlfriend ever get jealous of you being out there with all these swooning femmes in the heartland?

Lynn: Yeah, my girlfriend was pretty paranoid during our last U.S. tour. She was totally sure that I was sleeping my way across America, but I think now she feels pretty secure. She accepts that women are going to get crushes on me when they see me on stage doing the kind of shit that I do.

Lily: Does your butchness inspire a different reaction when you're on the street than when you're up on stage? Do you catch more shit in one circumstance or the other?

Lynn: On stage I don't get shit at all for the way I look. Most people that come to our shows are into punk rock — or if they're not, they're just totally blown away that I have the guts to be the way I am and not be ashamed of it. Either they're entertained by me, they think I'm funny, they want to be like me, or they're like, "that's more shocking than I've ever seen before!" I have a whole different personality on the stage, too. I feel totally powerful. I feel like I can do and say things that I could never say otherwise. I get to act out and do all kinds of stupid, ridiculous, obnoxious shit that I wouldn't do on the street.

It's way harsher on the street because it's a more mainstream environment. There have been times when I've been on the street, or on the train, with my girlfriend, and like four little frat boys will see us and start talking shit about dykes and saying (about my girlfriend), "Oh, what's she doin' with her? She must not like dick!" Just like totally harassing the fuck out of me — and I look the exact same way that I do on stage, except I have my shirt on!

Before when I was drunk, I'd walk up to guys like that and start a big fucking scream fest in their face, which would be really dangerous. I could've ended up super fucked up doing that shit, so now that I'm sober I try to think more about self-preservation. I have to think rationally and bite my tongue in that type of situation, especially around my girlfriend. She'll be like, "Don't say nothing. I'll handle it." She's a femme, and she knows how to rap boys, so she can handle them, while they're threatened by me because I'm too much like them.

Lily: Some butch women feel uncomfortable in their female body. Do you ever feel that way?

Lynn: I have. When I was younger, like seventeen or so, I was real hippy, and not in the political sense! I was bummed about that, so when I got into speed, the big thing was about body issues. I just thought, "Oh, I don't have to eat for days; I can just drink alcohol and lose all this weight and my hips will be boyish." I'd always wanted boyish hips. I feel more comfortable in my body when my hips are narrow. Now my body has grown into something that I like. Now my hips aren't so wide, and I'm more wiry.

I totally like my tits; my tits are great. They're just the right size, they're not too heavy, they don't weigh me down, and they conform to patriarchal standards of beauty. They're not as big as a *Playboy* centerfold's, but I like looking at 'em.

Lily: What about "Butch in the Streets"? Do you still do that song?

Lynn: I am constantly campaigning to do that song again. Sometimes the band gets bored with old songs like that one, because musically, they're too simple, and I say, revise the fucking music or whatever, cuz the lyrics are genius! That song is basically about me because the girl walks around all butch, wearing leather and combat boots and acting real aggressive all the time, studly and everything, but when she gets in bed she's a total pillow queen, a do-me queen.

Lily: And that's you?

Lynn: Yeah! I do love to throw my legs up. I'm a total helium heels.

Lily: Do you think there's a lot more butch bottoming going around than gets talked about?

Lynn: I always just assume there is! I try to call Flipper on it, like "C'mon, Flip, you know you want it, your butt wants it," and she's like, "Uh uh!" She's totally adamant that she never takes it, says she always pitches, she never catches.

Lily: Why do you think there's such resistance to being a butch bottom or to getting done?

Lynn: As a child, if you look around and see that all the people who are having fun and who have all the power are boys, you want to be a boy. So you try to imitate them in every way, even though you learn to hate them cuz they never accept you as one of them.

But you try to do everything they do — piss standing up, play football, fuck but not get fucked, or whatever it is. So I guess when you grow up you're still in that mode.

Lily: That boys, and girls who modeled themselves after boys, don't get fucked, you mean?

Lynn: Yeah, right. Especially in America where the homophobic bias against male penetration is totally blown into paranoid proportion!

Lily: When you were growing up, were you encouraged to be butch or were you groomed to be a girly-girl?

Lynn: I was raised to be a total girly-girl! Ruffles, petticoats, little white gloves, curlers, nail polish. Wendy Ward Charm School. Ballet school. I was like, "Gimme a drum set!" Nope! My parents sent me to ballet school instead.

My mom took me to a shrink when I was eight because I always wanted to climb trees, and I got kicked out of ballet school, and she wanted to figure out what the problem was. She thought I was going to be a dyke. I didn't realize that this was why I was going to see a shrink, but she took me and said, "Just go in there and talk to the nice man," and I was like, "OK, I always like to talk to people about myself, so, *fine*!" He asked me all these questions, and I said whatever, answered him.

When I came out as a dyke at the age of seventeen my mom said, "I knew it! I knew he was wrong! He told me you were going to be OK! And I knew he was just stupid, and that you were a total lesbian! I knew it then when you were eight years old!" And I was like, "Well, it must not have come as much of a shock to you then!"

Lily: If you were groomed to be a femme, who acted as a role model for you as a butch?

Lynn: My dad was the kind of dude I wanted to be, especially when he was young. He was a total babe. He was a surfer and an athlete, and all the chicks liked him, and I wanted to be like that.

When I got to be about twelve, I wanted to be like David Cassidy. He was sort of androgynous, yet sort of femme, and all the chicks liked him. He was a big heartthrob. I had my entire room plastered with David Cassidy posters. So while my family thought I was all into David Cassidy, I wanted to *be* him! But the real reason why I had to watch "The Partridge Family" every Friday night was not to see David Cassidy, but to see Susan Dey! I had a little picture of Susan Dey next to my bed, in with all the David Cassidy pictures, that I would totally kiss good-night every night.

Lily: Did you have any butch models in music?

Lynn: Patti Smith. She was pretty butch. But I was more into trying to emulate dudes. Like Jim Morrison. Ever since I was little, I would play air guitar in the mirror. When I was little it was the Beatles, when I was thirty, it was Black Flag. But I was always a dude. When I looked in the mirror and played those games, I saw myself as a boy.

Lily: Do you still?

Lynn: Yeah, I still do. But not to the point where I'm going to go get a sex change or anything. I'm used to my body, I'm dealing with it, plus I like to get plowed, so what the fuck, it serves me well. Psychologically, though, I've always viewed myself as a boy, aged anywhere from five to nineteen. A young boy, sensitive but boyish.

Lily: So how did all these childhood influences, from within and without your family, affect your view on being butch?

Lynn: I think that if you're going to have a kid, and you want that kid to be a certain way, you can't push it too hard because it might backfire. My mom really pushed femininity really hard, and shamed me if I didn't act the way she wanted me to: "How come you can't be like Dana? Look at her! She's in the sandbox with you all day, and her white dress is nice and clean and you're a mess. You're bad! How come you can't be like so-and-so? Bad, bad, bad...." She'd put me down for the way I walked: "You walk like a drunken sailor." All this shit that I believed for a long time. I believed I was bad, and I tried as hard as I could to fit in, even into my teens. 'Til I was seventeen I was wearing dresses, trying to go out with guys, fucking guys, listening to my mom saying, "You just haven't found the right one yet. Try a younger one, an older one, a European one...." I tried like ten guys and they were all yuck, boring.

I ended up rebelling against her and being pissed off. It took thirty years for me to be totally comfortable with my face without makeup, to be able to look at myself in the mirror without any eyeliner or anything and say, "That is OK." And when I realized that I had hated myself that much, I was so pissed off at my mom that I vowed I would never wear a dress again. If I wear one I feel like I'm wearing a sandpaper jumpsuit sandy side in.

I'm just now getting to the point where I can accept the feminine side of me again, the feminine side that I am recreating and allowing to be.

Lily: So is being butch and exploring your feminine side as you recreate it as much about rebellion as it is about revealing your true nature?

Lynn: Totally. But the more I get into the butch thing, the more I realize how scared I am to wear a dress, and how when I wear one, I feel like a fag in drag. All of this makes me question who I am even more. Who *was* I really? I try to go back to my childhood to find out what my natural tendencies really were. I try to look at the types of things that I did, and I look at the way I am in bed today. I have fantasies about being a straight girl getting plowed, all this shit. So why do I have this fucking problem about putting on a dress? Or putting on lacy lingerie and having my girlfriend do me? How come I can't look at myself in the mirror in my girlfriend's lingerie? Why am I so paranoid about that? Why can't I let anybody see that I have those desires?

I've always been this paradoxical amalgam. I'm a combination of opposites, and I need to be able to accept all of them. I've totally evolved — influenced by my environment, genetics, and social constructs, and I wonder who I'm going to become next.

BUTCH IN THE STREETS

Struttin' on an I-beam in her steel toes
and tool belt tellin' all the boys what to do
takes off her hard hat runs her hand through her crew-cut
but don't let all those muscles fool you.

She's a walkin' paradox in her jeans
and her Docs sportin' big ugly tattoos
she goes home throws her legs in the air
hopin' no one's heard the news.

She's butch in the streets, femme in the sheets
She's just a girl when she gets home
she wants to get plowed like anyone else
Don't let her fool you
She's femme to the bone

Walkin' down the street in her leather at night
you like the way she mounts
that Harley Davidson bike
jump on the back
she gives it a rev
don't think she's gonna top you
cuz she's belly up in bed

She's butch in the streets...

Butch Desire

PAT CALIFIA

FI**NALLY**, at the age of thirty-seven, I sometimes feel comfortable identifying myself as a butch when I am talking about my sexuality with other lesbians. Some of my hesitancy probably stems from coming out in the '70s when feminists seemed fiercely determined to wipe out any traces of '50s role-playing among gay women.

Self-identified butches and femmes have always been sexual outlaws. Straight society simply could not tolerate the idea of a feminine, "normal"-looking woman who got her needs for sex and masculine companionship and protection met by a strong and erotically skilled woman. Shrinks, cops, and fundamentalists have always hated butch women, who threaten male privilege by successfully competing with men for pussy and domestic caretaking.

But lesbian-feminism made butches and femmes outlaws in their own communities. For two decades, it's been anathema for most of us to say clearly, "I prefer a woman with broad shoulders and short hair who knows how to fuck," or "I want a woman who wears lipstick and looks hot in a little black dress that shows off her tits." If you asked a room full of lesbians to write down the names of all their friends and identify each of them as butch or femme, nobody would have trouble with that task, and there would be nearly complete agreement among all of the lists. But it's become more and more difficult for younger butches to learn how to strut their stuff from older bulldaggers, and femmes often have nobody to talk to about the ways that their sexuality and their relationships resemble and are different from those of heterosexuals.

Anti-sex feminist theory, homophobic precepts of modern psychology, and the fact that it's still illegal in many states for women to make love with other women have made lesbians paranoid about their own history and culture. It's very difficult to form a butch identity in this atmosphere of suspicion, paranoia, and sexual scarcity. We're afraid of butches because they draw attention to our existence, and some of us feel that as long as we are invisible we will be safe. Butch dykes who have some of the skills (sports, carpentry, martial arts) or personality traits (independence, physical courage, assertiveness) that are usually male prerogatives often make other women feel wimpy or cowardly. Most of us don't get enough sex, and we're angry with butches because there aren't enough of them to go around. And yet, our first response when somebody announces that she is butch (or would like to be) is punitive. We tell her, "You're not really butch."

I've been examining some of the myths that I've heard from other lesbians about butches. Some of these rules made sense back in the '50s. But I think we need to evaluate our stereotypes and make some new rules for role-playing. It's time to bring butch/femme into the '90s, or we'll never get what we're jonesin' for.

Real butches are supposed to be born, not made. And real butches are supposed to know how to make love to other women automatically, without instruction. This pair of myths sets butches up to compete with one another instead of being able to teach, support, or help each other. It also makes many of us extremely brittle about our act in the bedroom. A partner who asks us for something specific can make us nasty and defensive.

If you're really butch, you're never supposed to wear women's clothes. You're supposed to hide your female body, especially in bed. If you are a liberated butch, you might take your shirt off, but a surprising number of butches still leave all of their clothes (including their boots) on during sex.

These strictures are based on the idea that there is something shameful and inherently helpless about women's bodies. Butches (especially if they are identifiable as such during childhood) get told a lot that they are failures as women. We're told that we're ugly and clumsy. And we're often threatened with violence or abuse because "somebody needs to show you you're really just a girl." In addition to receiving these negative messages from the outside, many butches have their own uneasy feelings about being born into the wrong body. A fair number of female-to-male transsexuals try to alleviate their gender dysphoria by being butches.

The last thing we need is to have our sexual partners contribute to this self-hate. The fact that we are female is the basis for our value as beings who are sexually attractive to other lesbians. Other homosexual women want us because we are women who do some of the things that men do — only better. If you are ashamed of your own tits and your own cunt, I believe you will always be a little repelled by and somewhat contemptuous of femmes and jealous of their freedom to be both female and valued for their femininity.

When I came out, butches were never supposed to let their partners touch them. Either you didn't come at all, or you came during tribadism (rubbing your crotch against her leg). Today, a liberated butch might let her partner go down on her or touch her clit, but a real butch does not get fucked. If you aren't running the fuck and being in charge — if you want somebody else to do you or tell you what to do — your butch identity is liable to be revoked the second the Stone Butch Sex Police catch up with you.

Leather dykes can be credited with challenging these assumptions and making it possible for vanilla dykes to break out of the '50s mold. In fact, many butches and femmes try to join the leather community when they have little or no interest in S/M because S/M dykes talk more openly about sex and offer women more choices about how to structure their pleasure. In the long run, this is frustrating. If butches and femmes are ever going to get what they want, they need to start thinking of themselves as a sexual minority, speaking up about their lives, and creating a more visible subculture.

In the S/M community, deciding whether you are a top or a bottom is a separate process from deciding whether you're butch or femme. There are femme tops and butch bottoms, and there are also butches who enjoy crossdressing. If a leather butch bottom can be proud of being able to take her top's fist, pinstripe-suit butches should be able to get it up to do the same.

S/M dykes assume that a top should be rewarded by getting any type of sexual service she desires, whether that's a back rub, a blow

job, or a nice, hard fuck. Bottoms who don't know how to get a top off are stigmatized for being lazy and boring. Vanilla femmes, be warned. If you want to be a good time, you'd better own as many dildoes as you do pairs of high-heeled shoes.

Then there's the myth that a genuine butch only has sex with femmes. In the bars where I came out, butches went home with each other all the time, but they had to make shame-faced jokes about it the next day, punch each other in the arm, and say things like, "Well, we should have known two brothers couldn't figure out who should be on top," or "You can't play house with two daddies."

Once again, the lesbian S/M community has made butch-on-butch sex an acceptable option. Daddy/boy role-playing is, if anything, more popular than daddy/girl relationships. Leather butches often pair up to become fuck buddies or lovers. I don't see any reason why pool-playing butches who have no interest in ever owning a riding crop can't do the same thing. It's kind of like being a female faggot. If you want to have somebody big and strong who smells like men's cologne and cigars to snuggle you or take you to bed, you shouldn't have to put on a skirt or grow a ponytail to enjoy that privilege.

The last set of myths about "real" butches are the hardest to acknowledge, and they provide us with the best reason to lighten up and get a little more honest (and kinky!). Because a "real" butch allows other lesbians to make the rules for her and decide who's butch and who's not, because she denies her own cunt and sacrifices her own pleasure to get other women off, she is entitled to do some of the shitty and resentful things that men do. On the mild end of the scale, that means ridiculing women and being a sexist, misogynist asshole. But it can also include being physically abusive and violent. I believe that the taboo on butches getting their own sexual needs met also contributes to the alcoholism and drug abuse that is so painfully common in our community.

I didn't become a queer to serve other people's notions of propriety. I am a butch who sometimes likes to wear low-cut dresses. I prefer to bed other butches. I am not interested in having sex with women — butch or femme — who don't know how to fuck me. And if you think that means I'm not butch, just turn your back on me, darlin'. I can fix that attitude in a hurry.

PAT CALIFIA

ABOUT THE EDITORS

LILY BURANA is the editrix/publisher of the sexzine *Taste of Latex*. She is a bisexual femme, who is fond of masculine-identified beings, regardless of their plumbing. When she's not making porn or drooling over butch things, she publishes articles in *The Advocate, Hustler, LA Weekly, Maximum RocknRoll, Chic, Future Sex* and *On Our Backs*. She is writing a book about her life in the sex industry entitled *Punkstitute*.

ROXXIE grew her hair long after realizing that her male contemporaries had given up short hair. Now she can bond with her male art friends (and share long hair equipment). She publishes *Girljock*, the alternative sportwomen's magazine. A features writer, cartoonist and illustrator, Roxxie's comics appear in *Real Girl*. She is a devoted soccer enthusiast.

LINNEA DUE cut her hair short when she realized a lot of guys her age had abandoned their hippie dreds and were spending bucks at the style shop. She is the author of three novels, *High and Outside* (Harper & Row/Bantam/Spinsters Ink), *Give Me Time* (William Morrow/Berkeley) and *Life Savings* (Spinsters Ink). She is researching her first full length nonfiction work, *Joining the Tribe: Growing Up Gay and Lesbian in the '90s*, to be published by Doubleday in 1995.

Books from Cleis Press

LESBIAN STUDIES

Boomer: Railroad Memoirs
by Linda Niemann.
ISBN: 0-939416-55-7 12.95 paper.

**The Case of the
Not-So-Nice Nurse**
by Mabel Maney.
ISBN: 0-939416-75-1 24.95 cloth;
ISBN: 0-939416-76-X 9.95 paper.

Dagger: On Butch Women
edited by Lily Burana,
Roxxie, Linnea Due.
ISBN: 0-939416-81-6 29.95 cloth;
ISBN: 0-939416-82-4 14.95 paper.

**Daughters of Darkness:
Lesbian Vampire Stories**
edited by Pam Keesey.
ISBN: 0-939416-77-8 24.95 cloth;
ISBN: 0-939416-78-6 9.95 paper.

**Different Daughters:
A Book by Mothers
of Lesbians**
edited by Louise Rafkin.
ISBN: 0-939416-12-3 21.95 cloth;
ISBN: 0-939416-13-1 9.95 paper.

**Different Mothers: Sons &
Daughters of Lesbians Talk
About Their Lives**
edited by Louise Rafkin.
ISBN: 0-939416-40-9 24.95 cloth;
ISBN: 0-939416-41-7 9.95 paper.

**Girlfriend Number One:
Lesbian Life in the 90s**
edited by Robin Stevens.
ISBN: 0-939416-79-4 29.95 cloth;
ISBN: 0-939416-80-8 12.95 paper.

**Hothead Paisan: Homicidal
Lesbian Terrorist**
by Diane DiMassa.
ISBN: 0-939416-73-5 14.95 paper.

A Lesbian Love Advisor
by Celeste West.
ISBN: 0-939416-27-1 24.95 cloth;
ISBN: 0-939416-26-3 9.95 paper.

**Long Way Home: The
Odyssey of a Lesbian
Mother and Her Children**
by Jeanne Jullion.
ISBN: 0-939416-05-0 8.95 paper.

**More Serious Pleasure:
Lesbian Erotic Stories
and Poetry**
edited by the Sheba Collective.
ISBN: 0-939416-48-4 24.95 cloth;
ISBN: 0-939416-47-6 9.95 paper.

**The Night Audrey's
Vibrator Spoke: A Stone-
wall Riots Collection**
by Andrea Natalie.
ISBN: 0-939416-64-6 8.95 paper.

**Queer and Pleasant Danger:
Writing Out My Life**
by Louise Rafkin.
ISBN: 0-939416-60-3 24.95 cloth;
ISBN: 0-939416-61-1 9.95 paper.

**Rubyfruit Mountain: A
Stonewall Riots Collection**
by Andrea Natalie.
ISBN: 0-939416-74-3 9.95 paper.

**Serious Pleasure: Lesbian
Erotic Stories and Poetry**
edited by the Sheba Collective.
ISBN: 0-939416-46-8 24.95 cloth;
ISBN: 0-939416-45-X 9.95 paper.

SEXUAL POLITICS

**Good Sex: Real Stories
from Real People**
by Julia Hutton.
ISBN: 0-939416-56-5 24.95 cloth;
ISBN: 0-939416-57-3 12.95 paper.

**The Good Vibrations Guide
to Sex: How to Have Safe,
Fun Sex in the '90s**
by Cathy Winks and
Anne Semans.
ISBN: 0-939416-83-2 29.95 cloth;
ISBN: 0-939416-84-0 14.95 paper.

**Madonnarama: Essays on
Sex and Popular Culture**
edited by Lisa Frank and
Paul Smith.
ISBN: 0-939416-72-7 24.95 cloth;
ISBN: 0-939416-71-9 9.95 paper.

**Sex Work: Writings by
Women in the Sex Industry**
edited by Frédérique Delacoste
and Priscilla Alexander.
ISBN: 0-939416-10-7 24.95 cloth;
ISBN: 0-939416-11-5 16.95 paper.

**Susie Bright's Sexual
Reality: A Virtual Sex
World Reader**
by Susie Bright.
ISBN: 0-939416-58-1 24.95 cloth;
ISBN: 0-939416-59-X 9.95 paper.

**Susie Sexpert's Lesbian
Sex World**
by Susie Bright.
ISBN: 0-939416-34-4 24.95 cloth;
ISBN: 0-939416-35-2 9.95 paper.

FICTION

Another Love
by Erzsébet Galgóczi.
ISBN: 0-939416-52-2 24.95 cloth;
ISBN: 0-939416-51 4 8.95 paper.

**Cosmopolis: Urban
Stories by Women**
edited by Ines Rieder.
ISBN: 0-939416-36-0 24.95 cloth;
ISBN: 0-939416-37-9 9.95 paper.

**Dirty Weekend:
A Novel of Revenge**
by Helen Zahavi.
ISBN: 0-939416-85-9 10.95 paper.

A Forbidden Passion
by Cristina Peri Rossi.
ISBN: 0-939416-64-0 24.95 cloth;
ISBN: 0-939416-68-9 9.95 paper.

In the Garden of Dead Cars
by Sybil Claiborne.
ISBN: 0-939416-65-4 24.95 cloth;
ISBN: 0-939416-66-2 9.95 paper.

Night Train To Mother
by Ronit Lentin.
ISBN: 0-939416-29-8 24.95 cloth;
ISBN: 0-939416-28-X 9.95 paper.

**The One You Call Sister:
New Women's Fiction**
edited by Paula Martinac.
ISBN: 0-939416-30-1 24.95 cloth;
ISBN: 0-939416031 X 9.95 paper.

Only Lawyers Dancing
by Jan McKemmish.
ISBN: 0-939416-70-0 24.95 cloth;
ISBN: 0-939416-69-7 9.95 paper.

Unholy Alliances: New Women's Fiction
edited by Louise Rafkin.
ISBN: 0-939416-14-X 21.95 cloth;
ISBN: 0-939416-15-8 9.95 paper.

The Wall
by Marlen Haushofer.
ISBN: 0-939416-53-0 24.95 cloth;
ISBN: 0-939416-54-9 paper.

POLITICS OF HEALTH

The Absence of the Dead Is Their Way of Appearing
by Mary Winfrey Trautmann.
ISBN: 0-939416-04-2 8.95 paper.

AIDS: The Women
edited by Ines Rieder and Patricia Ruppelt.
ISBN: 0-939416-20-4 24.95 cloth;
ISBN: 0-939416-21-2 9.95 paper

Don't: A Woman's Word
by Elly Danica.
ISBN: 0-939416-23-9 21.95 cloth;
ISBN: 0-939416-22-0 8.95 paper

1 in 3: Women with Cancer Confront an Epidemic
edited by Judith Brady.
ISBN: 0-939416-50-6 24.95 cloth;
ISBN: 0-939416-49-2 10.95 paper.

Voices in the Night: Women Speaking About Incest
edited by Toni A.H. McNaron and Yarrow Morgan.
ISBN: 0-939416-02-6 9.95 paper.

With the Power of Each Breath: A Disabled Women's Anthology
edited by Susan Browne, Debra Connors and Nanci Stern.
ISBN: 0-939416-09-3 24.95 cloth;
ISBN: 0-939416-06-9 10.95 paper.

Woman-Centered Pregnancy and Birth
by the Federation of Feminist Women's Health Centers.
ISBN: 0-939416-03-4 11.95 paper.

LATIN AMERICA

Beyond the Border: A New Age in Latin American Women's Fiction
edited by Nora Erro-Peralta and Caridad Silva-Núñez.
ISBN: 0-939416-42-5 24.95 cloth;
ISBN: 0-939416-43-3 12.95 paper.

The Little School: Tales of Disappearance and Survival in Argentina
by Alicia Partnoy.
ISBN: 0-939416-08-5 21.95 cloth;
ISBN: 0-939416-07-7 9.95 paper.

Revenge of the Apple
by Alicia Partnoy.
ISBN: 0-939416-62-X 24.95 cloth;
ISBN: 0-939416-63-8 8.95 paper.

You Can't Drown the Fire: Latin American Women Writing in Exile
edited by Alicia Partnoy.
ISBN: 0-939416-16-6 24.95 cloth;
ISBN: 0-939416-17-4 9.95 paper.

AUTOBIOGRAPHY, BIOGRAPHY, LETTERS

Peggy Deery: An Irish Family at War
by Nell McCafferty.
ISBN: 0-939416-38-7 24.95 cloth;
ISBN: 0-939416-39-5 9.95 paper.

The Shape of Red: Insider/ Outsider Reflections
by Ruth Hubbard and Margaret Randall.
ISBN: 0-939416-19-0 24.95 cloth;
ISBN: 0-939416-18-2 9.95 paper.

Women & Honor: Some Notes on Lying
by Adrienne Rich.
ISBN: 0-939416-44-1 3.95 paper

ANIMAL RIGHTS

And a Deer's Ear, Eagle's Song and Bear's Grace: Relationships Between Animals and Women
edited by Theresa Corrigan and Stephanie T. Hoppe.
ISBN: 0-939416-38-7 24.95 cloth;
ISBN: 0-939416-39-5 9.95 paper.

With a Fly's Eye, Whale's Wit and Woman's Heart: Relationships Between Animals and Women
edited by Theresa Corrigan and Stephanie T. Hoppe.
ISBN: 0-939416-24-7 24.95 cloth;
ISBN: 0-939416-25-5 9.95 paper.

To Place an Order

Since 1980, Cleis Press has published progressive books by women. We welcome your order and will ship your books as quickly as possible. Individual orders must be prepaid (U.S. dollars only). Please add 15% shipping. Pennsylvania residents add 6% sales tax. Mail orders to Cleis Press, P.O. Box 8933, Pittsburgh PA 15221. **MasterCard** and **Visa** orders: include account number, expiration date, and signature. **Fax** your credit card order to (412) 937-1567. Or, **phone** us Monday–Friday, 9am–5pm Eastern Standard Time at (412) 937-1555.